Present Yourself 1

SECOND EDITION

Teacher's Manual

D1288098

CAMBRIDGE
UNIVERSITY PRESS

Steven Gershon

CAMBRIDGE
UNIVERSITY PRESS

University Printing House, Cambridge CB2 8BS, United Kingdom

One Liberty Plaza, 20th Floor, New York, NY 10006, USA

477 Williamstown Road, Port Melbourne, VIC 3207, Australia

314–321, 3rd Floor, Plot 3, Splendor Forum, Jasola District Centre, New Delhi – 110025, India

79 Anson Road, #06–04/06, Singapore 079906

Cambridge University Press is part of the University of Cambridge.

It furthers the University's mission by disseminating knowledge in the pursuit of education, learning and research at the highest international levels of excellence.

www.cambridge.org
Information on this title: www.cambridge.org/9781107435834

First edition 2008
Second edition 2015
Reprinted 2018

Printed in Italy by Rotolito S.p.A.

ISBN 978-1-107-43583-4 paperback Teacher's Manual 1 with DVD
ISBN 978-1-107-43563-6 paperback Student's Book 1

Additional resources for this publication at www.cambridge.org/presentyourself

Contents

Plan of the Student's Book

	Knowing your audience	Planning a presentation
Getting ready pages 2–7	Completing a lifestyle survey with classmates Talking about your presentation experiences	Learning about the steps for presentation planning Brainstorming, selecting, and organizing information for a presentation

Unit	Exploring the topic	Focusing on language	Organizing ideas
1 **A good friend** pages 8–19	Talking about people's personal profiles Completing a personal profile questionnaire about yourself and a classmate	Describing a friend's personality, interests, and activities Completing an activities survey about classmates	
2 **A favorite place** pages 20–31	Describing different kinds of places Interviewing classmates about favorite places	Talking about favorite places Talking about activities people do in their favorite places	
3 **A prized possession** pages 32–43	Discussing what makes possessions important to people Completing a survey about classmates' possessions	Describing prized possessions Explaining the history and use of a possession	All units focus on: Brainstorming, selecting, and organizing information into a presentation outline Watching or listening to a complete model presentation
4 **A memorable experience** pages 44–55	Talking about different types of experiences and feelings Interviewing classmates about their experiences	Describing a memorable experience Setting the scene and using time expressions to describe an experience	
5 **I'll show you how** pages 56–67	Discussing different types of skills and talents Survey classmates about their skills and talents	Demonstrating how to do or make something Presenting the materials you need and giving instructions	
6 **Screen magic** pages 68–79	Quizzing your classmates about their movie and TV knowledge Talking with classmates about favorite movies and TV shows	Speaking about popular movies and TV shows Describing types of movies and their features	

Developing presentation techniques	Giving your presentation
Using gestures, making eye contact, maintaining posture, managing anxiety, and projecting your voice	Planning and giving a self-introduction

Adding impact	Developing presentation techniques	Present yourself!
Learning about the parts of a good introduction and conclusion Learning about openers and closers	Making effective note cards Using eye contact to connect with an audience	Planning and giving a presentation about a good friend
Beginning a presentation with a general statement about people Ending a presentation with an invitation	Making gestures for descriptions Using body language: posture and hand position	Planning and giving a presentation about a favorite place
Beginning a presentation with a question Ending a presentation by emphasizing why your topic is special	Showing an object to an audience Using-show-and-tell expressions to point out the features of an object	Planning and giving a presentation about a prized possession
Beginning a presentation with a "mystery" list Ending a presentation by "passing the mike"	Projecting your voice, speaking clearly and avoiding fillers Using stress to emphasize intensifiers	Planning and giving a presentation about a memorable experience
Beginning a presentation with problem-raising questions Ending a presentation with a "call to action"	Making gestures for actions Checking understanding when giving instructions	Planning and giving a demonstration how to do or make something
Beginning a presentation with an interesting fact Ending a presentation with a recommendation	Using sentence stress for content and function words Pausing between phrases	Planning and giving a review about a movie or TV show you have seen

Introduction

About the book

Present Yourself is a presentation skills course for adult and young adult learners of English. The course combines careful language control and well-supported, communicative activities with a process approach to giving presentations. In this way, *Present Yourself* offers students an opportunity to develop the important life skill of speaking clearly and effectively about a topic of interest to an audience. *Present Yourself 1, Experiences* is intended for low-intermediate students (CEFR A2/B1 level) and focuses on giving presentations about everyday experiences. It can be used as a main text in a presentation skills course, in the context of a general conversation course, or as a component in speaking or integrated-skills classes.

Online resources and DVD

www.cambridge.org/presentyourself

All video material for *Present Yourself* can be downloaded from the *Present Yourself* website. Subtitles are available for all video to fully support students. The video material is available on the DVDs that accompany this Teacher's Manual. An identical audio-only version is available on the website and on the DVD for any teachers not using the video. The website also contains a range of photocopiable support.

Structure of the course

Present Yourself has six main units and one introductory unit. The *Getting ready* introductory unit acquaints students with the process of planning a presentation, and it offers an entry point to giving a presentation by having students give a short self-introduction. Each of the six main units guides students through the entire presentation process with engaging speaking activities and focused viewing or listening activities. These activities provide relevant topic input and clear functional language support, targeting both vocabulary and useful sentence patterns. Moreover, the core of each unit provides a complete model presentation that students use to help them construct their own presentations.

Process approach

Present Yourself follows a carefully designed process approach, which recognizes that an effective presentation is the result of an individualized process, involving a number of linked stages. The teaching emphasis is placed on guiding students through the presentation process step by step. The basic elements of this process are, to a large degree, responses to a sequence of essential questions: *What do I talk about? Who is my audience? What language and vocabulary do I need for this topic? How do I select and organize relevant information and ideas? What techniques will enhance the delivery of my presentation?* And finally, *What changes should I make so my presentation is better next time?*

The aim of this process approach is to provide students with a set of transferable tools within a practical framework that will help them to brainstorm, prepare, organize, deliver, and evaluate their own presentations, whatever the topic and purpose. To this end, each unit focuses on a specific presentation topic and guides students through the entire presentation process, lesson by lesson, thereby continually reinforcing the steps and making the framework more and more familiar.

Topics

The six main units of *Present Yourself 1* focus on topics that encourage students to speak from their personal experience. The units are loosely graded by level of difficulty, ranging from introducing a friend in Unit 1 and describing a memorable experience in Unit 4 to reviewing a movie or TV show in Unit 6. However, as we all know, every class is different, so feel free to pick and choose units according to your students' interests, class level, and available time.

Unit organization

Getting ready

Getting ready is an introductory unit, which gives students an opportunity to get to know their classmates so they will feel more comfortable when they give their presentations in class. The activities also help students think about the steps in the process of planning a presentation. Students watch or listen to a simple model of a self-introduction presentation and are gently guided through the process of planning their own self-introduction presentations, which they practice and then give in small groups.

How a unit works

Each main unit contains six lessons to guide students through the process of building an effective and engaging presentation. Following the initial **Exploring the topic** lesson of a unit, each lesson builds on the previous one in order to provide students with the set of skills needed to create and deliver their own presentations.

Exploring the topic

This lesson helps students to think about the topic and what they already know about it. The activities introduce useful topic-based vocabulary and encourage students to interact with one another through surveys, questionnaires, quizzes, and interviews. When students finish this lesson, they will have generated ideas that they can use later in the unit as they begin to plan their own presentations.

Focusing on language

This lesson highlights useful target expressions and sentence patterns that naturally occur when talking about the unit topic. Students watch or listen to different speakers using the target language in the context of a presentation and complete structured language-based tasks. Students then consolidate the target language through a clearly structured speaking activity with the support of a useful-language box.

Organizing ideas

In this lesson, students see how ideas can be selected from a brainstorming map and organized into a presentation outline. Students are first asked to notice which ideas from a brainstorming map have been included as main topics in an outline. Then they complete the outline with additional notes. Finally, students have an opportunity to watch or listen to the complete model presentation as they check the completed outline. All of the model presentations

appear in a section at the back of the book in a reader-friendly format.

Adding impact

This lesson focuses on the elements of a strong introduction and conclusion, which add impact to a presentation. While watching or listening to the introduction and conclusion of the unit's model presentation, students complete a cloze task which targets the specific type of opener and closer that the speaker uses. They then practice using the opener and closer in a clearly structured speaking task.

Developing presentation techniques

At this stage of the unit, students are ready to focus on specific presentation techniques related to the actual delivery of their presentation. Each unit introduces two useful presentation techniques, including the use of note cards, making eye contact, gesturing for emphasis, and projecting the voice. In every unit, students watch or listen to speakers using the presentation techniques; students then practice these techniques with a partner or in a group.

Present yourself!

In the last lesson of the unit, students plan, organize, and give their own presentations based on the unit topic. First, students brainstorm ideas for their topic and create an outline for their presentation. Then they add an introduction and conclusion, including an opener and closer. Finally, they practice on their own before giving their presentations to the whole class or in a group. Each unit also offers helpful note card and PowerPoint tips that students can try out. A self-evaluation form for each unit is included at the back of the book for students to assess their own presentations.

Extension and support materials in the Student's Book

Following all of the main units in the Student's Book, there are three sections of materials that extend and support student learning. These are:

Expansion activities (pages 80–91)
Model presentations (pages 94–100)
Self-evaluation forms (pages 102–106)

Expansion activities

The **Expansion activities** give students additional input and practice in the language and skills from each unit. The double-page set of activities for each unit features a range of viewing activities and a final unit goals checklist for students to assess their achievement of the unit's goals (shown on the first page of each unit). The viewing activities generally focus on openers and closers from the **Adding impact** lesson, the two target skills from the **Developing presentation techniques** lesson, using note cards, and using PowerPoint. The note card and PowerPoint activities expand on the tips in the **Present yourself!** lesson. Each unit recycles video from the main unit to reinforce students' learning, and contrasts it with re-recorded "bad" models to raise students' awareness of what to do and what *not* to do.

The **Expansion activities** section has been designed for students to do on their own as self-study in their own time outside class. In each unit's **Expansion activities**, one of the characters from the main units (Ben, Grace, Patrick, Emma, Jason, or Sophie) acts as the guide on the video: they introduce the viewing activities and then follow up by giving the answers and a brief explanation. This means that teachers who are pressed for time covering the main unit's activities in class do not need to devote time, energy, or lesson planning for the expansion activities. However, for teachers with enough time and the necessary classroom technology, all or some of the expansion activities can be incorporated into the classroom lessons whenever appropriate. Below are a few possible ways to use the activities in the course.

Ways to use extension activities

1 Independent homework

- At the beginning of Unit 1, introduce students to the **Expansion activities** section on pages 80–91. Point out the overview boxes at the top of pages 80, 82, 84, 86, 88, and 90 and explain that for each unit, one of the characters from the book will be their guide on the video to introduce the activities and explain the answers.

- Tell students that the expansion activities will give them more practice of what is covered in the main units, which will help them to give better presentations.

- Explain that they can do the expansion activities for each unit whenever they have time: they can decide themselves when to do them. However, they should try to complete all the expansion activities before planning and giving their own presentation at the end of each unit.

2 Teacher-guided homework

- At the beginning of Unit 1, introduce students to the **Expansion activities** section on pages 80–91. Point out the overview boxes at the top of pages 80, 82, 84, 86, 88, and 90 and explain that for each unit, one of the characters from the book will be their guide on the video to introduce the activities and explain the answers.

- Tell students that they will get more out of the expansion activities if they do them as follow-up to the related unit activities covered in class. Assign specific expansion activities as homework after students have completed the relevant unit activities during the lesson.

- When covering a unit, assign or suggest the relevant expansion activity at the end of the lesson in which students complete the related unit activity or tip.

3 Classwork

- At the beginning of Unit 1, introduce students to the **Expansion activities** section at the back of the book. Point out pages 80–91 and give them an overview of this section, as provided above.

- Tell students that you will often or occasionally do the expansion activities in class as part of the lessons.

- When covering a unit in class, ask students to turn to the relevant expansion activity at the back of the book after they complete the related unit activity or tip.

- View the expansion activity with students, stopping occasionally to offer guidance, further explanation, or to answer questions.

- Have students check or compare answers in pairs or small groups, before eliciting answers.

Depending on available time and technology, you may decide during the course to combine all three planning options. In this way, for selected units, you may have students do the expansion activities in their own time as they wish (Option 1); for some units you may assign specific expansion activities at certain times (Option 2); and for other units, you may do the expansion activities with the students during the lesson (Option 3).

To use as homework assessment, you may want to have students occasionally show you their student's book to check off that they have done the expansion activities. Alternatively, you could ask students to photocopy the relevant expansion activities pages and submit them as homework.

Model presentations

Each unit, including the *Getting ready* unit, includes a complete presentation that the students can watch or listen to as a useful model for planning their own presentation on the unit topic. All of the model presentations appear on pages 94–100 in an attractive, colorful, reader-friendly format. Each model presentation page highlights the introduction, body, and conclusion sections of the presentation to reinforce the structure of an effective presentation emphasized throughout the course.

All video and audio material is available from the *Present Yourself* website (www.cambridge.org/presentyourself), so students can watch or listen to the model presentations on their own as necessary. Subtitles are available for all video material to provide additional support for students. At times, you may also want to have students look at the model presentation during a lesson to highlight specific vocabulary, sentence patterns, or openers and closers. In addition, especially for lower-level classes, you could have students look at the model presentation while watching or listening to the presentation if they are having difficulty with listening comprehension.

Self-evaluation forms

The **Self-evaluation** forms on pages 101–106 of the Student's Book may be used at the end of each unit after students have given their presentations. These forms allow students to reflect upon and evaluate their own presentations in terms of preparation, content, and delivery. Students complete a simple checklist and write comments about what they did well and what they want to improve for their next presentation. Although the forms are intended for students' own use, you could have students photocopy and submit the completed form to you, so you can respond with your own written comments. It is also useful to

have students look back at the **Self-evaluation** form from the previous unit before they begin planning each successive presentation.

Course planning and flexibility

Present Yourself has been designed to be used in a variety of teaching situations. The six main units in each level are arranged roughly in order of gradually increasing challenge, both in terms of language and presentation skills. However, the presentation topic of each unit is completely independent of other units and can easily stand alone. Therefore, although it may be ideal to cover all the units in order, feel free to cover the units in any order you think will most benefit your class. Moreover, if you have limited time, large classes, or lower-level students who need more time to fully cover a unit, you can skip over any units that you don't have time to cover. You may also choose to have students study only the **Developing presentation techniques** lesson of units that you don't have time to cover fully in class. This would give students the complete range of presentation skills that they can use for the presentation assignments you choose to include.

Lesson planning

Each main unit of *Present Yourself* represents a series of linked lessons, beginning with **Exploring the topic** and ending with the **Present yourself!** lesson. For 90-minute classes, if each unit lesson is covered fully in class, it will take five to six class periods to bring students to the point where they can prepare and give their own presentations based on the unit topic. However, every class is different in terms of the interests and levels of students as well as the available time for the course. Therefore, *Present Yourself* offers the flexibility to increase or decrease the amount of time spent on each unit. This can be done in a number of ways:

Expanding the time spent on each unit

- Incorporate some or all of the **Expansion activities** into the class lessons while working through the unit.

- Have students submit their presentation outlines or even a full first draft of their presentations for feedback from you or their classmates before giving their presentations. This will effectively add a useful revising or editing phase or lesson to the presentation process.

- When working on the final **Present yourself!** lesson, have students complete all the brainstorming, planning, and preparation for their presentations during lesson time. This will allow you to oversee and offer help during the entire planning phase. You could also spend some time during this lesson reviewing the presentation skills from the **Developing presentation techniques** lessons in previous units.

- Once students have completed the planning and preparation for their presentations during the **Present yourself!** lesson, set up a "rehearsal" lesson, during which students can practice their presentations in small groups. This will allow students to get informal feedback from their classmates, make changes to the content, and work on their delivery before giving their presentations more formally in front of the whole class.

- Video all or a select number of student presentations. One simple way to do this is to ask students with a smartphone to video presentations from designated classmates. Then, after students have given their presentations, set up a post-presentation evaluation session, with students watching selected presentations while you elicit their perceptions of the main strengths and weaknesses of the presentations as a whole. Alternatively, this follow-up evaluation session could be done from memory, without video, either as a whole-class activity or in small groups, with each group reporting back to the class at the end of a discussion period.

Limiting the time spent on each unit

- Students have access to all of the video and audio material through the *Present Yourself* website. This means that you can assign all or some of the viewing or listening activities in each unit for homework. If you do this, you can then briefly go over the answers during the lesson before moving on to that lesson's speaking activities.

- With students at a higher proficiency level, skip one or more of the activities in the **Exploring the topic** and **Focusing on language** lessons. These two lessons can then be combined and covered in one class period instead of two.

- Have students do the **Organizing ideas** lesson (completing the brainstorming notes and presentation outline) as homework. Then, in the next class period, briefly check students' answers before moving on to the speaking activity (Exercise 2C) and the **Adding impact** lesson.

- While covering the final **Present yourself!** lesson, have students do either some or all of their presentation planning as homework. This means that students will complete the **Developing presentation techniques** lesson in class, and then in the next class period students will give their presentations.

- Any or all of the student presentations may be done in small groups of four to six students rather than in front of the whole class, one student at a time. For example, with a class of 30 students, there could be five groups doing their presentations at the same time. This means that the whole class could complete their presentations within one lesson, still allowing time for a follow-up feedback session. This format makes detailed grading and feedback for each individual student more difficult. However, you may choose to do the presentations in one or two of the units in this format, while giving more detailed individual feedback and grades to each student for the remaining presentations that they do in front of the whole class.

General teaching tips

Maximizing English in the classroom

Although *Present Yourself* focuses on developing students' presentation skills, it is also important to see the course goals within the context of improving students' general communicative competence. Many of the activities, particularly in the **Exploring the topic** and **Focusing on language** lessons, directly address these communicative aims. However, there are also many other opportunities during a lesson to maximize and extend the students' functional use of English. Aside from using English as much as possible for simple classroom instructions, explanations, and procedures, you can encourage students to use English when asking you for language help and when talking to one another while doing activities. A good way to do this is to provide some useful classroom expressions at the beginning of the course and then spend a little time getting students to practice them. Here are some examples:

Getting help:
What does . . . mean?
How do you spell . . . ?
How do you pronounce this word? How do you say . . . in English?
Can we watch/listen to it again, please?
Can you turn the sound up, please? (I can't hear it.)

Finding a partner for pair work:
A: *Do you have a partner?*
B: *No, not yet.*
A: *OK, let's work together for this activity.*

Forming groups:
A: *We need one/two more in our group.*
B: *OK, can I join your group?*

Comparing answers:
A: *What did you get for question number . . . ?*
B: *I got . . . How about you?*
A: *I got . . . , too.* Or *I don't know the answer.*

Deciding the timing for activities

It is difficult to suggest how long activities may take to complete as every class is different. Therefore, the timing of each activity is flexible, depending on the program syllabus, the level and interest of students, and your goals as a teacher. Activities can be shortened if necessary, or extended by using all the optional Lead-in and Follow-up tips offered in the unit teaching notes. In general, it is helpful to let students know how much time they will have to complete an activity, and then to let them know when they have one or two minutes left.

Giving students thinking time

When new material or a new activity is introduced, learners need time to process language and come up with their own ideas before they can be expected to respond. This is particularly important for lower-level or less confident students. The unit teaching notes always suggest that you read the activity instructions aloud first. This is to give students

time to absorb what they are being asked to do. It is also a good idea to give students enough time to look at the pictures, scan the questions or information in charts, digest the language in boxes, or read the model language before asking them to carry out the activity or respond orally. By being attentive to students' facial expressions and body language, you will usually know when most of the class has had enough time to absorb the material and is ready to move on with the activity.

Using visuals (pictures) to activate schema

The Student's Book contains many pictures that introduce the topic of each unit. Visuals can go a long way in helping students to activate their schema, that is, to build on their background knowledge about the topic. This is especially important during brainstorming and planning stages, as well as before viewing or listening activities. It is always helpful to give students a few minutes to take in a picture fully, mentally describe what is in the picture, and then share their ideas with a partner. There are many suggestions in this Teacher's Manual for exploiting the pictures in the classroom.

Checking answers in pairs

The unit teaching notes often suggest that students share their answers with a partner before you elicit answers from the whole class. This will help to create a more interactive and collaborative class atmosphere. It will also allow lower-level students to be on a more equal footing when you elicit answers from the whole class, especially for viewing or listening activities. The first few times students do this, you may want to refer them to the relevant functional expressions from the **Maximizing English in the classroom** section above.

Modeling activities and language

To help students understand and respond to activities, the unit teaching notes often ask you to model the activity or target language. The purpose is not to give students sentences to memorize, but rather to show them how to do the activity. Modeling an activity with one of the higher-level students in the class is an efficient way to demonstrate how an activity works. Showing is always more effective than telling. As the saying goes, "A picture is worth a thousand words."

Forming pairs and groups

Many of the activities in the Student's Book are for pairs or groups. Students should not always work with the same partner or group. Instead, manage the speaking activities so that students move around and talk to different classmates. Getting students to talk to many different classmates will not only help reinforce their English but also make the lessons more interesting. One way to have students change partners is simply to have every other row of students turn around to face the row behind. Or you can have students rotate in different directions. If students are seated around a large table, they can simply rotate positions around the table. You may also have students simply stand up and move around the room to find a new partner who is not normally seated near them. The first few times students do this, you may want to refer them to the relevant functional expressions from the **Maximizing English in the classroom** section above.

If an activity requires pairs or even-numbered groups, but there is an odd number of students in the class, have one student share the role of another student, each taking turns to respond to their partner. Alternatively, you could be the partner of the extra student, though this will make monitoring other students more difficult.

Monitoring and helping

The unit teaching notes frequently suggest that teachers "walk around the classroom, helping students as necessary" while they are engaged in an activity. This serves several purposes:
1. It makes sure students remain on task in English.
2. It helps individual students, pairs, or groups that are having difficulty.
3. It gives you a sense of when most of the students have finished an activity.
4. It allows you to make a mental note of which students will be able to give an acceptable response if you call on them to share their answers with the class after they have finished the activity.

To monitor effectively, it's a good idea to move around the classroom, sitting or standing near pairs or groups and checking (as unobtrusively as possible) that they are doing the activity correctly and using appropriate language. If students are working too slowly or having difficulty expressing themselves, you can briefly join in the pair or group activity, offering suggestions. Alternatively,

you can pause the activity to explain or model the activity again before moving on to a new pair or group. You may also choose to keep notes, in a notebook or on a seating chart about the strengths and weaknesses of particular students in case they need extra help. You could also jot down notes about particular activities for future course planning.

Asking for volunteers

The unit teaching notes frequently suggest that the teacher ask for volunteers to give answers to viewing or listening activities, share their ideas with the class, or report back what they found out about a classmate after a questionnaire, survey, or interview activity. As we all know, students can be reluctant to volunteer, especially in a large class, so a little gentle persuasion is sometimes necessary. Of course, one effective form of persuasion is the student's grade. At the beginning of the semester when you are explaining your grading system, you may want to point out the importance of participation, which includes volunteering answers, ideas, opinions, and information when you ask for it. You could explain that a percentage (for example, 10 percent) of their final grade will be based on participation.

When students in a class are consistently reluctant to volunteer, it is tempting to quickly call on a non-volunteering student to give answers. All teachers know the dangers of that: wasting class time as a weak or unprepared student fumbles for an inadequate or wrong answer, embarrassing the student in front of their classmates, making them even less likely to volunteer in the future, and creating an uncomfortable classroom environment, which is demotivating for everyone. However, it is sometimes necessary to call on non-volunteering students when no hands go up, or when the same few students volunteer every time. At those times, reading students' body language and facial expressions can be a great help in determining who is likely to give an acceptable response. Even more valuable is making a mental note of those students while monitoring the activity (see **Monitoring and helping** above).

Using note cards

When making a presentation, students often try to memorize their full presentation. This is understandable, especially when speaking in a second language. However, if they forget one small part, or even a few words, of their script, they can quickly become paralyzed, with their mind completely blank, while they silently try to remember what comes next.

To avoid this frightening situation, students often want to write out the full text of their presentation on a piece of paper, word for word, to have in front of them when they are presenting. Once again, this is understandable. However, when students have the complete word for word text in front of them, they tend to read out large chunks of the text from the paper – with their eyes cast down, locked onto the paper instead of the audience. Moreover, their voice takes on a monotonous, flat, "reading" intonation that effectively puts the audience to sleep.

Present Yourself, therefore, emphasizes the benefit of making and using effective note cards when students present. In Unit 1, the **Developing presentation techniques** lesson focuses on note cards and eye contact. Then, in each of the following units, specific note card tips are given in the **Present yourself!** lesson that are relevant to the presentation topic of that unit. Finally, most of the **Expansion activities** include a note card task. Speaking from notes is a valuable skill, and the more students practice this skill, the more comfortable they will be with it and the more effective their presentations will be.

PowerPoint

PowerPoint has become a standard visual tool used in a wide variety of presentation contexts. Therefore, many of the model presentations in *Present Yourself* include the use of PowerPoint. PowerPoint tips also appear on the last page of every unit, and several viewing activities focusing on PowerPoint are included in the **Expansion activities** section at the back of the book.

However, many classrooms do not have the necessary technology to allow PowerPoint to be used, and you may feel that your students' time and energy is better spent focusing on target language, organization, and speaking skills. PowerPoint is therefore not necessary for any of the student presentations in this course. If the use of PowerPoint is inappropriate for your teaching situation, you may want to simply point out the PowerPoint tip in the **Present yourself!** lesson and tell students that the tips and expansion activities will be useful for future presentations they may need to do for other classes, events, and occasions.

Dealing with nerves

Almost everyone gets nervous when speaking in front of a group. This is natural, even for native speakers. Students will most likely be a little anxious at the beginning of the course, especially if they don't know each other very well. It is therefore vital to create a comfortable, nonthreatening, collaborative learning environment, with a lot of encouragement and praise for the students' efforts. You can also help to decrease this initial anxiety by doing some ice-breaking "get to know you" activities in the first few lessons. This will lighten the class atmosphere and encourage students to view their classmates as a supportive audience for their presentations. *Getting ready*, the introductory unit of *Present Yourself*, contains ice-breaking activities to serve this purpose. You are also encouraged to add your own favorites. In addition, the **Developing presentation techniques** lesson in *Getting ready* includes a few tips to manage anxiety.

When it comes time to give their presentations, most students will no doubt suffer some stage fright. There are a number of ways to help students deal with this:

- Make sure students realize that some nervousness is completely normal when speaking in public. Have students practice their presentations in small groups first, allowing them to build confidence by practicing in an informal environment.

- Deep breathing can also be used to help decrease nervousness. Taking a few deep breaths silently just before beginning to speak is a great way to calm nerves and start with a strong voice. When students are preparing their first presentation, have them practice walking to the front of the room, facing the class, and taking two or three deep breaths before saying their first sentence. A simple reminder to take a few breaths before each presentation should help students deal with nerves.

- Have students stand up straight with a confident posture and practice making eye contact with their classmates. A confident posture translates into a confident speaker.

- Encourage students to speak slowly and calmly. When nervous, people tend to speak quickly, as if they want to finish as soon as possible. Having students practice speaking calmly also helps reduce nervousness.

- Depending on your students' personalities, you may also want to encourage them to add a little humor to their presentation. Getting some smiles or a laugh from the audience toward the beginning of a presentation does a lot to calm nerves and build confidence. Humor is a great icebreaker!

- Most important, let students know at the beginning of the course that good, solid preparation and practice is the very best way to decrease their nervousness about presenting. The more prepared they are, the more confident they will feel presenting to an audience. Remind them to practice, practice, then practice some more!

How to use this Teacher's Manual

This Teacher's Manual contains the following materials:
- Step-by-step teaching notes for each unit in the Student's Book
- Language summaries
- Outline worksheets
- Peer evaluation form
- Assessment form
- Video/audio scripts for all recorded viewing or listening activities

Unit teaching notes

The Teacher's Manual unit begins with a brief overview, describing the aims of each lesson of the corresponding Student's Book unit. In addition to detailed teaching instructions for each activity, the unit teaching notes contain lists of useful vocabulary and language that students will encounter in the activities as well as helpful tips for lead-in and follow-up activities, specific grammar points, and cultural references. Answers for all exercises are also provided.

Language summaries

There is one photocopiable **Language summary** for each corresponding unit in the Student's Book (pages 71–76). These summaries list the important words, phrases, and expressions from each lesson as well as helpful language students will need to use in their presentations. You may want to hand out a copy of the unit's **Language summary** to each student before you begin the **Present yourself!** lesson in each unit.

Encourage students to review the vocabulary and to refer to the helpful language as they plan their presentations.

Outline worksheets

The photocopiable **Outline worksheets** on pages 77–82 of this Teacher's Manual are designed to be used in class while students are giving their presentations. Students take notes on their classmates' presentations, which allows them to engage actively in the presentations as they listen. The worksheets help students focus on the content of the presentations, and the process of taking notes helps students listen intently for details and retain the information they hear. Each worksheet follows the same structure as the planning outline in the **Present yourself!** lesson of the corresponding Student's Book unit, so students will be familiar with the organization and topics.

Using the Outline worksheets

- Before students give their presentations, decide how many worksheets each student will complete. You may want to limit the number to two or three presentations.

- Have students draw names to decide which classmates' presentations they will take notes on. Alternatively, allow students to choose the presentations on their own.

- Hand out the appropriate number of copies of the worksheet to each student in the class.

- Have students read the topics on the worksheet and explain that they should complete the outline with details from the presentation as they listen. After the presentation, they should complete the last section of the worksheet: "Something else I'd like to know about the topic."

- Collect the worksheets after all students have given their presentations. You may want to hand them back with written comments and count them as an in-class assignment or a participation grade.

Peer evaluation form

The photocopiable **Peer evaluation form** on page 83 is designed to be used in class after students' presentations to give them a chance to learn from the process of assessing their peers' work. It also provides students with an opportunity to receive helpful feedback from their classmates.

Using the Peer evaluation form

- At the beginning of the class period in which students will give presentations, assign each student two classmates' presentations to evaluate. Make sure each student in the class will receive evaluations from two other classmates.

- Hand out two copies of the form to each student.

- Have students read the criteria on the form, and explain that they should listen carefully to their assigned classmate's presentation and then complete the form.

- Have students give their completed forms to the appropriate classmates after all the presentations are finished. You may want to check the **Peer evaluation forms** yourself before students give them to the presenters.

- Encourage students to read their evaluations and to keep them for future reference.

Assessment form

The photocopiable **Assessment form** on page 84 is designed to help you evaluate students' presentations as you watch them in class. The form is divided into the three main areas, which students focus on as they progress through each Student's Book unit: preparation, content, and delivery. You can use the form either as a formal assessment tool or to provide students with informal written feedback.

Using the Assessment form

- Before students give their presentations, make one copy of the form to assess each student in the class.

- Familiarize yourself with the criteria on the form.

- As you watch students' presentations, mark the score for each section accordingly (1 = lowest score; 5 = highest score).

- Calculate and write the score out of a possible 50 points in the space provided.

- Use the section at the bottom of the form at the end of each presentation to summarize each student's strengths and make suggestions for future improvements.

- If you choose to assign a formal grade to the presentation, multiply each student's point score by 2 to calculate a percentage. For example, if a student's score is 41, 41 x 2 = 82 percent.

Student's Book video and audio scripts

The video and audio scripts on pages 85–101 of this Teacher's Manual correspond to the viewing or listening activities in the *Getting ready* unit, the six main units, and the **Expansion activities** in the Student's Book.

For the *Getting ready* and six main units, the audio is identical to the video and is available to any teachers who prefer not to use the video. For the **Expansion activities**, there is no separate audio as these are designed to be viewing activities. Before doing a viewing or listening activity with students, you may want to preview the scripts so that you can readily answer any questions students may have about the language or content presented. These pages are photocopiable, and you may hand them out to students for in-class or at-home study whenever you feel them to be useful. The full scripts are also available via the subtitles option on all video clips.

In conclusion

I do hope you enjoy teaching *Present Yourself 1, Experiences* and that your students find the topics and activities in this course both interesting and useful. Becoming an effective, confident presenter is a long-term process, but I am sure that by the end of the course, your students will be making effective, engaging presentations that they can be proud of and that their audiences will enjoy.

I would be happy to receive any comments about *Present Yourself* that you or your students would like to share.

Steven Gershon

Getting ready

Overview

The activities in the four lessons of this introductory unit guide Ss to the main goals of learning how to plan a presentation and giving a 1–2 minute self-introduction.

Lesson	Activities
Knowing your audience	Conducting a class survey to find out about classmates' background and lifestyle Talking with classmates about their presentation experiences and attitudes
Planning a presentation	Ordering the steps involved in effective presentation planning Seeing how ideas are brainstormed and organized for a self-introduction Watching or listening to Maricel's self-introduction
Developing presentation techniques	Learning about five important presentation techniques: using gestures, maintaining good posture, making eye contact, managing anxiety, projecting your voice
Giving your presentation	Brainstorming and organizing ideas for a self-introduction Giving a 1–2 minute self-introduction to the class or in a group

Knowing your audience

Pages 2–3

Lead-in

As Ss are often a little nervous and apprehensive at the beginning of a presentation skills course, you may want to begin by giving the Ss an overview of the course and a brief, encouraging pep talk.

Overview

You could include any of the following points:
- how many presentations the Ss will do during the semester or year
- what kinds of presentations they will do (have Ss look at the contents page)
- how many lessons they will usually have to plan and prepare their presentations
- how long the presentations will be (average 3–5 mins.)
- how the Ss will be graded for the presentations and the course

Pep talk

- It's very normal to be nervous about giving a presentation – especially in a foreign language. A useful quote: *There are only two types of speakers in the world: the nervous and liars.* (Mark Twain)
- Ss will learn how to brainstorm ideas, organize information, and make an outline for a presentation. These steps will make their planning much easier.
- Ss will also learn a lot of useful techniques for developing their presentation skills.
- Ss will have a lot of opportunities in every unit to talk to their classmates and practice the skills they are learning.
- If Ss work hard, prepare well, and help each other, the atmosphere in the class will make it much easier for them to stand up at the front of the room and speak with confidence to their audience.
- With hard work and lots of practice, all Ss will be able to give a good presentation. A useful quote: *All the great speakers were bad speakers at first.* (Ralph Waldo Emerson)

Alternatively, you could have the Ss look at *To the student* on page ix and read it aloud as you expand with the points above.

1 Lifestyle survey

Vocabulary

abroad: in a foreign country

instrument: an object, such as a piano, guitar, or flute that is used to play music

nervous: worried or a bit frightened

pet: an animal, like a dog or cat that is kept in the home as a companion

A

- Tell Ss that in this course, their classmates will be their audience. Explain that it is useful for Ss to know some information about the audience before giving a presentation, so that they can choose topics that match the audience's needs and interests. The activities in this lesson will help Ss get to know their classmates.
- Have Ss open their books to page 2. Read the instructions aloud.
- Have Ss read the items in the *Find someone who* column and explain any unfamiliar language.
- Point out the model answer in the chart and the question starters at the bottom of the page.
- Make sure Ss understand that they will need to stand up and move around the classroom asking their classmates the questions. If someone answers no, they can ask the classmate a different question or ask a different classmate the question. At the end of the activity, each S should have six different names.
- Have Ss stand up and move around the room, asking their questions.
- Walk around the room, helping Ss as they complete the activity.
- When Ss have all or most of the chart filled in, ask Ss to sit down.

Tip

☐ For lower-level classes, before having the Ss move around the room, elicit from Ss the correct question form for each item and write it on the board. Also elicit one or two example follow-up questions for a few of the items in the chart. For example: *What instrument do you play? How long have you played it? What countries have you visited? When did you go? How long were you there? What pet do you have? How long have you had it? What's its name?*

☐ In this kind of whole-class "melee" activity, some Ss may be a little shy to seek out other Ss who are not speaking to someone. If there are two Ss in different areas of the room who are both on their own not speaking to anyone, pair them up.

☐ If you are limited for time, but are fortunate to have a very outgoing, talkative class of Ss, tell Ss to ask only one follow-up question for each interview topic.

B

- Read the instructions aloud.
- Have Ss look at the notes they wrote for their classmates' answers and choose something interesting they found out about two or three of their classmates.
- Point out the model language at the bottom of the page.
- Ask for a few volunteers to tell the class what they found out.

2 Presentation experience questionnaire

Vocabulary

aspect: a part or feature of something

confident: feeling sure about yourself and your abilities

gesture: a movement of the body, hands, or arms to show an idea or feeling

pounding: beating (moving) fast and hard

somewhat: a little

A

- Tell Ss that they will now talk about their presentation experiences and attitudes toward giving presentations.
- Read the instructions aloud.
- Have Ss read the questions in the questionnaire themselves or read them aloud. Explain any unfamiliar language.
- Have Ss form pairs. Make sure they understand that for Questions 3–6 they should make notes of their partner's answers because they will use the information later.
- Walk around the classroom, helping pairs as necessary as they do the activity.

B

- Read the instructions aloud. Have pairs join together to form groups of four.
- Give Ss time to look at their notes of their partner's answers.
- Walk around the classroom, helping pairs as necessary as they do the activity.
- Ask for a few volunteers to tell the class what they found out about their partner.
- Tell Ss that they are now going to learn to plan a presentation step by step.

□ If Ss need more practice, have pairs join up with a different pair and repeat the reporting back about their partner.

□ End the activity by taking an informal survey of the class for Questions 1, 2, and 5 by asking Ss to raise their hands.

Planning a presentation

Pages 4–5

1 Presentation steps

Vocabulary

attention-getting: something that makes you see, listen, or notice

body: the middle or main part of a presentation, which includes most of the information about the topic

brainstorm: note down a lot of ideas for an activity very quickly before thinking about them carefully

detail: fact or item of information about a topic, subject, or person

outline: a set of notes that shows the main topics and facts, written in preparation for a presentation

A

- Read the instructions aloud. Tell Ss that each S in the picture is working on a different step in planning a presentation.
- Have Ss form pairs.
- Walk around the classroom, helping pairs as necessary as they share their ideas.
- Elicit ideas from Ss and write them on the board.

1A Possible answers

Seiji:	practicing his presentation with a note card
Haewon:	brainstorming ideas with a brainstorming map
Mila:	writing her introduction
Ian:	making note cards to use when he gives his presentation

B ◀))▶1

- Tell Ss to think about the best order to do the planning steps from Exercise 1A.

- Read the instructions aloud, along with the six steps. Explain any unfamiliar language.
- Have Ss order the six steps on their own, then compare their guesses with a partner.
- Play the video or audio once or twice as necessary while Ss check their guesses.
- Have Ss check the answers with a partner before eliciting answers from the class.
- If necessary, play the video or audio again to confirm the answers.

1B Answers

1	5	3	4	6	2

2 Brainstorming

Vocabulary

nickname: an informal short name which is often used by friends and family to show affection

A

- Tell Ss they are going to see how a student planned a self-introduction presentation.
- Read the instructions aloud. Tell Ss to notice that Maricel didn't put into her brainstorming map two of the topics she first wrote down.
- Have Ss mark their answers.
- Elicit answers from Ss and correct as necessary.

2A Answers

Topics included: My names; My hometown; My family; This class

B

- Tell Ss that after Maricel made her brainstorming map, she thought of more information to include in her self-introduction.
- Read the instructions and additional notes aloud.
- Walk around the classroom, helping Ss as necessary while they complete the map.
- Have Ss compare their answers with a partner before eliciting answers from Ss.

2B Answers

Hometown: on an island; has beautiful beaches, delicious mangos

Family: Dad a fisherman; two brothers and two sisters

Greeting and my name: nickname Mar (for friends and family)

3 Organizing

A

- Tell Ss that Maricel has decided which topics and information to include in her self-introduction. Now she needs to organize the topics into the order she wants to talk about them.
- Read the instructions and information in the four note cards aloud.
- Have Ss number the note cards, then compare with a partner.
- Elicit answers from Ss to see if there is general agreement in the class.

B 🔊 ▶ 2

- Read the instructions aloud.
- Play the video or audio once or twice as necessary while Ss check their guesses.
- Have Ss check the answers with a partner before eliciting answers from the class.
- If necessary, play the video or audio again to confirm the answers.

Tip

If Ss have trouble following Maricel's presentation, have them look at the full presentation on page 94 while they watch or listen again.

3B Answers

Hometown	2	Name	1
Class goals	4	Family	3

Developing presentation techniques

Page 6

Vocabulary

anxiety: nervousness or fear

apologize: tell someone that you are sorry

maintain good posture: stand up straight

make eye contact: look directly into another person's eyes

shout: say something in a very loud voice

sway: move slowly from side to side

technique: a way of performing a skillful activity

tip: a useful piece of information or advice

A

- Tell Ss they are going to learn about some useful presentation techniques, like the ones that Maricel uses in her self-introduction.
- Tell Ss that when they give a presentation, the content – what they say – is very important. Explain that it is also very important to pay attention to the delivery of the presentation – how they say it. Good presenters use all of the techniques in the box to get their message across and make their presentations clear and interesting.
- Have Ss look at the pictures while you read the instructions aloud.
- Walk around the classroom, helping Ss as necessary as they write their answers.
- Have Ss compare answers in pairs before eliciting answers from the class.

A Answers (clockwise from top)

Use gestures
Maintain good posture
Project your voice
Make eye contact
Manage anxiety

B 🔊 ▶ 3

- Read the instructions and tips aloud. As you read each tip, demonstrate it as appropriate.
- Make sure Ss understand that in each set of three tips, one tip is wrong.
- Have Ss write their answers, then compare with a classmate.
- Play the video or audio once or twice as necessary.
- Have Ss check their answers in pairs before eliciting answers from the class.
- If necessary, play the video or audio again to confirm the correct answers.
- Finish by telling the Ss that they are now ready to plan their own self-introduction.

Giving your presentation

Page 7

A

- Tell Ss they are going to prepare and give a 1-minute self-introduction presentation. Then read the instructions aloud.
- Point out the brainstorming map and tell Ss they can decide what information to put in their self-introduction. If Ss need help, have them look back at Maricel's brainstorming map on page 5.
- Walk around the classroom, helping Ss as necessary while they complete the map.

B

- Tell Ss that a lot of preparation and practice is important for a good presentation. However, they don't need to memorize every word. They should use note cards with the main points and keywords.
- Read the instructions aloud.
- Give Ss time to complete their notes. Encourage them to write brief notes and keywords rather than complete sentences or a complete script.
- Walk around the classroom, helping Ss as necessary.

C

- Read the instructions aloud.
- Point out the model language for the introduction and conclusion.
- Walk around the classroom, helping Ss as necessary while they complete their introduction and conclusion.
- Allow time for Ss to practice on their own or with a partner.

D

- Read the instructions aloud.
- Point out the note card tip. If possible, demonstrate the tip with a note card.
- Have Ss form groups. Point out the reminder at the bottom of the page.
- Tell Ss to enjoy finding out about each other.

1 A good friend

Overview

All of the activities in the six lessons of Unit 1 guide Ss to the main goal of planning and giving a 3–5 minute presentation to introduce a good friend to their classmates.

Lesson	Activities
Exploring the topic	Talking about people's personal profiles Completing a friendship questionnaire with a classmate
Focusing on language	Learning words to describe people Talking about interests and activities
Organizing ideas	Seeing how to brainstorm ideas and create an outline for a presentation introducing a friend Watching or listening to Sophie's model presentation introducing her friend Kate
Adding impact	Focusing on the parts that make a good introduction and conclusion Getting an overview of various types of openers and closers
Developing presentation techniques	Making and using effective note cards Making eye contact to connect with an audience
Present yourself!	Brainstorming and organizing ideas for a presentation to introduce a friend Giving a presentation to a group or the class

Exploring the topic

Pages 8–9

Vocabulary

blogging: writing an online diary or a commentary that people can read on the Internet

easygoing: someone not difficult to get along with; who doesn't get angry or upset often

hang-out spot: place where people like to spend time alone or with friends (spot = place)

have something in common: share interests or have similar characteristics

hometown: city or town where a person grew up; may be different from their birthplace

house, techno: styles of electronic music often played at clubs

Man United: Manchester United football club in England

messy: untidy, disorganized

nerdy (adj; noun = **nerd**): very interested in intellectual, scientific, technical, or computer-based activities; often shy in social situations

nest: the home that birds make in a tree from twigs and branches; slang for home

occupation: job

outgoing: friendly, sociable, likes meeting and being around people

personal profile: a description of someone containing the most important facts about them

quotation (**quote**): a common or well-known saying taken from a person or book

FriendNet Profiles

Page 8

Lead-in

Books closed. Ask Ss some or all of these questions:

➤ *How many social networking sites (SNS) do you use?*

➤ *On which ones do you have a profile?*

➤ *What types of information do people usually include about themselves on SNS (e.g., names, hometowns, hobbies and interests, occupations)?*

➤ *How many friends do you have on the SNS you use?*

➤ *Have you every made new friends on SNS that you have never met in person?*

A

■ Have Ss form pairs and tell them to open their books to page 8.

■ Read the instructions aloud and direct Ss' attention to the quote, *Birds have nests; humans have friendship.*

■ Make sure Ss understand *nest*. Have them discuss the quote.

■ Ask a few pairs to share their ideas with the class.

1A   Possible answer

I think friendship is like a bird's nest because they both give warmth, safety, security, and protection.

B

■ Have Ss stay in their pairs from Exercise A.

■ Read the instructions aloud and give Ss time to read the profiles.

■ Ask Ss to underline any words they don't know.

■ Clarify the meaning of any unknown words or get Ss to look them up.

■ Allow time for Ss to discuss what they have in common with the people on FriendNet.cup.

■ Ask a few volunteers to share their responses with the class.

2 **Friendship questionnaire**

Vocabulary

get along with: feel comfortable with someone; have a good relationship with someone

---

A

■ Have Ss form new pairs – at the beginning of the course it's a good idea for Ss to talk to as many different classmates as possible.

■ Read the instructions aloud.

■ Have Ss read the questions silently. Give them a minute to think about their answers.

■ Have pairs decide who will ask first and who will answer first.

■ Remind Ss to give a few details, not just one-word answers.

■ Remind Ss to write notes for their partner's answers.

■ Walk around the classroom, helping Ss as necessary.

B

■ Combine pairs to form groups of four.

■ Read the instructions aloud.

■ Point out the model language at the bottom of the page.

■ Give groups a few minutes to share their information.

■ Call on a few volunteers to share something interesting about a classmate.

Focusing on language

Pages 10–11

1 **Personalities**

Vocabulary

laidback: calm and agreeable; easygoing

messy: opposite of neat and tidy

moody: a person whose feelings change often

workaholic: someone who works a lot and finds it difficult not to work

---

Usage note

workaholic: This is normally used as a noun, e.g., *He's a workaholic.* Other similar terms are *alcoholic* and *chocoholic.*

A

Lead-in

Books closed. Elicit some adjectives for describing people's personalities and write them on the board. Have Ss tell you which words, in their opinion, are positive, negative, or neutral.

■ Tell Ss to open their books to page 10.

■ Read the instructions aloud.

■ Read the words aloud to describe people in the box and have Ss repeat them.

■ Point out the example answer, then have Ss write their answers.

■ Direct Ss to compare with a partner, then elicit answers from volunteers.

1A Answers

2	neat and tidy	5	adventurous
3	funny	6	active
4	night people	7	quiet and serious

B

- Have Ss write in their own adjectives for personality traits in the box.
- Have Ss compare with a partner.
- Elicit words from a few volunteers and write the words on the board.
- Clarify meanings as necessary.

Follow-up

Arrange Ss into pairs. Have Ss try to think of synonyms (words with similar meaning) and antonyms (words with opposite meaning) for the words in the box in Exercise 1A.

C ◄))) ► 4

Lead-in

Ask Ss to look at the photos of Nick, Hana, and Sami and guess or predict some of their personality traits, interests, hobbies, etc.

- Read the instructions aloud.
- Have Ss read the information for Nick, Hana, and Sami.
- Play the video or audio and have Ss circle their answers.
- Ask Ss to check their answers in pairs.
- Call on a few Ss to share their answers.
- Confirm answers by watching or listening again.

1C Answers

Nick: junior high school; different; quiet and serious; messy; music

Hana: part-time job; similar; outgoing; adventurous; meeting people

Sami: 3 years; similar; active and energetic; funny; outdoor sports; telling jokes

Follow-up

Ask Ss to tell a partner which of the three friends (Nick, Hana, or Sami) they are most similar to in personality, interests, likes, and dislikes.

2 My friends

A

- Tell Ss to think about their own friends.
- Read the instructions aloud and point out the example answers in the chart.
- Have Ss complete the chart individually.
- Walk around the classroom, helping Ss as necessary.

B

- Have Ss form pairs.
- Read the instructions aloud and point out the model language on the page.
- Allow time for Ss to share the descriptions of their friends.
- Ask a few volunteers to share their descriptions with the class.

3 Interests and activities

Vocabulary

triathlon: a sports contest with three different events, usually cycling, swimming, and running

A

Lead-in

Books closed. Ask Ss to write down the most common or popular activities that friends their age do together. Have Ss compare their lists with a partner. Then elicit some activities from Ss and write them on the board.

- Ask Ss to open their books to page 11. Read the instructions aloud.
- Read the words and phrases from the box aloud and ask Ss to repeat them.
- Allow time for Ss to complete the box individually. Then have them compare in pairs.
- Call on a few Ss to share the words they wrote. Add them to the words already on the board.

B ◄))) ► 5

- Read the instructions aloud.
- Have Ss read the information for Patrick, Emma, and Jason.
- Play the video or audio and have Ss check their answers. Make sure Ss understand that they should check two interests for each speaker.
- Have Ss compare their answers in pairs.
- Call on a few Ss to share their answers with the class.

3B Answers

Patrick: going to blues clubs; going to classical concerts

Emma: singing karaoke; trying new restaurants

Jason: training for a triathlon; talking at a coffee shop

C ◄))) ► 5

- Read the instructions aloud.
- Play the video or audio and have Ss write their answers.
- Have Ss compare their answers in pairs.
- Call on a few Ss to share their answers with the class.
- Have Ss watch or listen again to confirm the answers as necessary.

4 Activities survey

Grammar point

- ◆ With the verb *play*, the article *the* is used with musical instruments, but not with games. For example: *play tennis / sports / the piano*
- ◆ Note that the verb *play* is generally used with competitive sports, but other activities use the verbs *do* or *go*. For example: *do exercise/judo, go skiing/surfing*.

A

- ▪ Read the instructions aloud and point out the written example in the chart.
- ▪ Tell Ss to interview three classmates and complete the chart. Encourage Ss to stand and move around the classroom so that they have a chance to speak to different classmates.
- ▪ Walk around the classroom, helping Ss as necessary.

B

- ▪ Read the instructions aloud and point out the model language.
- ▪ Allow time for Ss to think of what they want to say about the classmates they asked.
- ▪ Ask for a few volunteers to share what they found out about their classmates.

Organizing ideas

Pages 12–13

1 Sophie's brainstorming map

Tip

- ☐ As this is the first full unit Ss will do, we recommend spending some time orienting Ss to this **Organizing ideas** lesson. Explain that the activities are designed to guide Ss through the process of brainstorming and organizing information to include in a presentation. Also, point out that Ss will use the same process when they prepare their own presentation at the end of the unit.

☐ It may also be useful at this stage to explain to Ss that *brainstorming* means thinking of a large number of ideas in a short period of time. The goal in brainstorming is not to produce *good* ideas, but rather *any* ideas. In other words, at this stage, the goal is quantity, not quality. Later, the best, most useful ideas are selected from the brainstorming list.

Vocabulary

habits: activities people repeat daily or weekly

only child: a person without any brothers or sisters

reading tastes: the types of books, magazines, etc., people like to read. Also, *musical tastes, taste in movies*, etc.

A

Lead-in

Books closed. Have Ss close their eyes and picture their room at home and the things in it. After a minute, ask Ss to open their eyes. Ask Ss to raise their hand if they think a visitor could get a good idea about their personality and interests by looking at their room.

- ▪ Have Ss look at the pictures while you read the instructions and question aloud.
- ▪ Elicit several responses to the questions.
- ▪ Tell Ss they are going to find out more information about Kate in this lesson of the unit.

B

- ▪ Read the instructions aloud.
- ▪ Explain to Ss that the topics and details in the brainstorming map are for the body or main part of the presentation. Sophie will think about the introduction and conclusion later.
- ▪ Allow time for Ss to read the topics in the brainstorming map and look at the outline on page 13. Explain any unfamiliar language.
- ▪ Elicit answers from Ss.

2 Sophie's presentation outline

Vocabulary

street fashion: loose, baggy clothes, often worn by people who are into hip-hop music

optimistic: being cheerful and confident about the future; opposite = **pessimistic**

Tip

Before doing Exercise B, give a brief introduction to the presentation outline by explaining the following:

☐ The presentations are organized into three parts: an introduction, a body, and a conclusion.

☐ The main topics are represented by capital letters: A, B, C, etc.

☐ Smaller points and details are represented by numbers or bullet points.

A

- Explain to Ss that Sophie thought of a few more things to say after she made her brainstorming map.
- Read the instructions aloud.
- Allow time for Ss to read the additional notes and look at the outline. Explain any unfamiliar language.
- Have Ss complete the outline.
- Walk around the classroom, helping Ss as necessary.
- If Ss have been working individually, have them work in pairs to compare their answers.

B 🔊 ▶ 6

- Read the instructions aloud.
- Play the video or audio and have Ss check their answers.
- Elicit answers from Ss and clarify as necessary.

2B Answers

B **Things in common**: mothers are elementary school teachers; positive, optimistic; like to wear street-style clothes

C **How we are different**: smart, top student; only reads music magazines; Kate sleeps until noon on weekends; me up at 8 a.m.

D **What we do together**: twice a month hip-hop dance class near campus

If the above activity is difficult for Ss, have them watch or listen to Sophie's presentation again while looking at the complete model presentation on page 95. Alternatively, if using the video, turn on the subtitles.

C

- Have Ss form pairs or small groups.
- Point out the model language at the bottom of the page.
- Allow time for Ss to ask and answer the questions.
- Ask for a few volunteers to share what they found out about their partner or group members.

Adding impact

Pages 14–15

Tip

Before beginning this lesson, explain the following to the class:

In the last lesson, we focused on brainstorming and organizing ideas for the body, or main section, of a presentation. However, just like a good essay, a presentation also needs a strong beginning and ending to be complete. Now we are going to learn what goes into a good introduction and conclusion as well as some different ways to begin and end a presentation.

Vocabulary

make/have an impact: produce a strong effect on someone or something

remind: tell someone something again, to make sure they remember it

signal: an action, movement, or sound that gives information, e.g., a traffic signal

1 Introduction and conclusion

Tip

☐ Read the initial explanation and question aloud.

☐ Have Ss close their books or cover Exercise A with a piece of paper so they can come up with their own ideas.

☐ Elicit ideas from Ss.

A

- Read the instructions aloud.
- Focus Ss' attention on the eight parts of the introduction and conclusion. Clarify as necessary.
- Have Ss read the statements in the second column. Clarify as necessary.
- Point out the example answer.
- Have Ss complete the exercise individually.

- Walk around the classroom, helping Ss as necessary.
- Have Ss compare their answers with a partner, then elicit answers from volunteers.

B
- Read the instructions aloud.
- Point out the example answer.
- Have Ss complete the exercise individually.
- Walk around the classroom, helping Ss as necessary.
- Have Ss compare their answers with a partner, then elicit answers from volunteers.

Tip

Of course, good introductions and conclusions don't always contain every part that appears in Exercises A and B or in exactly the same order. Effective speakers vary what they put into the introduction and conclusion and where they place them. However, as the saying goes, one should know the rules before breaking them. For Ss at this level, it is sensible to present initially an "ideal" introduction and conclusion, which will work for most any type of presentation.

C
- Read the instructions aloud.
- Have Ss complete the activity individually.
- Walk around the classroom, helping Ss as necessary.
- Have Ss compare their answers with a partner, then elicit answers from volunteers.

2   Openers

Lead-in

Books closed. Ask Ss to imagine that they are going to watch or listen to many short presentations. Tell them that every speaker begins with "*Hello. Today, I will tell you about my good friend . . .*" Ask Ss to imagine how they will feel after four or five speakers (very bored, or asleep!). Tell Ss that good speakers always try to think of an interesting way to begin their presentation so they can get the audience's interest quickly.

- Read the explanation and the types of openers in the box aloud. Clarify as necessary.
- Tell Ss that each unit in *Present Yourself* will focus on one type of opener, so that by the end of the course they will know several different ways to grab the audience's attention.

A
- Read the instructions aloud.
- Have Ss complete the activity individually.
- Walk around the classroom, helping Ss as necessary.
- Have Ss compare their answers with a partner, then elicit answers from volunteers.

B ◀ ▶ 7
- Read the instructions aloud. If necessary, have Ss look again at Sophie's outline on page 13.
- Play the video or audio once or twice, as necessary, as Ss write their answers.
- Have Ss check their answers with a partner, then elicit answers from volunteers.
- Write the correct answers on the board for Ss' reference.

C

- Read the instructions aloud and make sure Ss understand the quotations and proverbs.
- Read aloud the expressions in the language box.
- Have Ss form pairs and complete the activity. Remind them to use the language from the box.
- Ask for a few volunteers to share their introduction with the class.

Follow-up

- Ask Ss if they know any quotations or proverbs about friends/friendship in their language or culture.
- Elicit answers from Ss and write them on the board.
- If Ss have Internet access, have them do a search for "quotations about friendship."
- Write any suitable quotations on the board.
- Have Ss do Exercise C again, using the new quotations/proverbs.

3 Closers

- Read the explanation aloud.
- Tell Ss that a good speaker always tries to end a presentation with a strong final statement. This helps the audience remember the topic and main points.

A

- Read the instructions and the types of closers in the box aloud. Clarify as necessary. Make sure that Ss understand that *mike* means *microphone*. Mime the idea of passing the mike while explaining that it means giving someone else the opportunity to speak.
- Have Ss complete the matching activity.
- Walk around the classroom, helping Ss as necessary.
- Have Ss compare their answers with a partner, then elicit answers from volunteers.

B 🔊 ▶ 8

- Ask Ss if they remember what type of closer Sophie used. Elicit suggestions from volunteers.
- Play the video or audio once or twice, as necessary, as Ss write their answers.
- Have Ss check their answers with a partner, then elicit the answer from a volunteer.

Follow-up

Tell Ss that each unit in *Present Yourself* will focus on one type of closer, so that by the end of the course they will know several different ways to make a memorable final impression on the audience.

Developing presentation techniques

1 Note cards

- Read the explanation aloud.
- Ask Ss to raise their hand if they have given a presentation or speech before. Ask those who have if it was difficult for them to remember everything they wanted to say. Ask Ss if they tried to memorize their presentation or speech. Finally, ask what they think the main problem is with memorizing a speech or presentation. (**Possible answers**: It takes a lot of time. It's easy to forget something when you're nervous. If you forget a word or sentence, you can "freeze" and not be able to remember anything.)

Vocabulary

extreme sports: sports that are dangerous, e.g., paragliding, kitesurfing, skydiving

outdoors: outside in fresh air, not inside a building or room

A

- Read the instructions aloud. Have Ss look back at pages 10–11 to remind themselves of Jason's presentation, as necessary.
- Tell Ss to read Sophie's and Jason's notes.
- Point out the note card tips.
- Make sure Ss understand that each line has a pair of either/or statements and that they should check only one statement for each pair.
- Have Ss complete the activity.
- Walk around the classroom, helping Ss as necessary.

1A Answers

Sophie: uses postcard-size cards; writes only main points and keywords; writes large; writes short phrases; uses bullet points; uses colored pens

Jason: uses A4 paper; writes out whole presentation; writes small; writes complete sentences; writes in paragraph form; writes in black ink only

B

- Read the instructions aloud.
- Have Ss form pairs and compare their answers.
- Elicit answers from volunteers.
- Make sure Ss understand why Jason's card is not so effective or useful. (**Answer:** with so much small block writing on the card, it is difficult to find your place if you forget what comes next.)

1B Answer

Sophie's note cards are more effective. They focus on the main points and keywords; they use a bold and colored font to make them easy to read.

Practice

- Read the instructions aloud.
- Tell Ss to use Sophie's cards as a model.
- If Ss have colored pens/pencils with them, they should use them. If not, bold, caps, and underlining can be used for highlighting.
- Allow time for Ss to rewrite Jason's notes.
- Walk around the classroom, helping Ss as necessary.
- Have Ss compare their note cards in pairs or small groups.
- If time permits, share a few of the best examples with the class.
- Tell Ss that they will get a lot of practice making and using effective note cards during the course.

2 Eye contact

Lead-in

Books closed. Tell the class that you are going to tell them about a good friend. Then speak for a minute or two, giving some information about when and where you met, what you have in common, how you are different, what you do together, etc. While you're talking, don't make much eye contact with the Ss. Instead, look down, look up, look over their heads, etc. When you finish, ask the Ss what they noticed about your presentation. Try to elicit that you did not make good eye contact (e.g., *Did I look at you much? Where was I looking most of*

the time?). Then ask Ss how they felt while you were speaking. Try to elicit that not making eye contact made them feel less attentive to your words and less interested in what you were saying.

A

- Read the instructions aloud.
- Have Ss form pairs and share their ideas.
- Walk around the classroom, helping Ss as necessary.
- Elicit answers from volunteers.

2A Possible answers

Patrick: Looking up at the ceiling while thinking what to say next

Sophie: Holding a note card in front of her face

Grace: Holding the note card too low so she has to look down to read it.

B

Vocabulary

at random: by chance; without a plan

lighthouse: a tower containing a light to guide ships at night. The light normally moves very smoothly to cover a large area.

master: become very skillful (an expert) or knowledgeable in an activity or subject

- Read the instructions and the tips in the box aloud.
- Direct Ss' attention to the descriptions under the tips.
- Have Ss complete the matching activity individually.
- Walk around the classroom, helping Ss as necessary.
- Have Ss compare their answers in pairs.
- Elicit answers from volunteers.

2B Answers

F Don't look at the ceiling or floor when you are thinking of what to say next. Just look at the space between people.

E This position makes it easy for you to move your eyes from your notes to the audience without moving your head too much.

A Look down at your notes for a maximum of 10 percent of your presentation time. This means practice, practice, practice!

B Don't read directly from your notes. When you need to check your notes, pause briefly, look at your notes, and then look up at the audience and continue speaking.

C Don't move your eyes left and right too evenly. It's better to look at all sections of the audience at random.

D Look at someone for three or four seconds. Then look at someone else when you begin the next sentence.

Practice

- Read the instructions aloud.
- Allow time for Ss to read the text about Sara silently, or read it aloud.
- Have Ss fold a separate sheet of paper to the size of a postcard.
- Allow time for Ss to make their note card.
- Walk around the classroom, helping Ss as necessary.
- Have Ss form small groups. Tell Ss that they can decide who they want to talk about – Sara or Sami.
- Have each group member give their mini-presentation using their note cards. You may want to have Ss stand up when they speak in their group.
- Point out the reminder and encourage Ss to make eye contact when they speak.
- Walk around the classroom, observing the Ss' presentations.
- Ask a few volunteers to do their mini-presentation for the class.
- Tell Ss that they are now ready to begin planning their own presentations.

Present yourself!

Pages 18–19

1 Brainstorm

Tip

In all of the units, depending on your available class time and student level, the planning activities in this lesson can be completed partially or fully as homework. However, as this is the first presentation Ss will do, we recommend spending some time going over the two pages of this lesson and having Ss complete some or most of the planning process in class. This will allow you to answer any questions they may have.

- Read the assignment and instructions aloud.
- As a reminder, have the Ss look again at Sophie's brainstorming map on page 12.

- Allow time for Ss to partially or fully complete their brainstorming maps. Encourage Ss to include information and details that they think their classmates will find interesting.
- Walk around the classroom, helping Ss as necessary.

2 Organize

- Read the instructions aloud.
- Have Ss look again at Sophie's outline on page 13, as necessary.
- Point out that Ss can add their own topics (*Other information*) wherever they think they fit best into their outline.
- Give Ss time to think of a presentation title and complete the outline.
- Walk around the classroom, helping Ss as necessary.

Tip

If Ss need more help organizing their outlines, collect the outlines and give written feedback on them to the Ss.

3 Add impact

- Tell Ss that the above outline is for the body of their presentation. It's time to think about the introduction and conclusion to make the presentation complete and balanced.
- Read the instructions aloud.
- Elicit or remind Ss what type of opener and closer Sophie used in her presentation. (**Answers:** quotation; comment about the future.) If necessary, have Ss look back at pages 14–15 and the model presentation on page 95.
- Allow time for Ss to complete their notes for the introduction and conclusion or ask Ss to complete them at home.

Tip

☐ Have Ss look at the model presentation on page 95. Ask them to underline the key language Sophie uses for her opener, topic statement, preview, conclusion signal phrase, review, and closer.

☐ Encourage Ss to use the Internet to find interesting quotations, sayings, or proverbs about friends or friendship. Alternatively, to save time, bring a list of suitable quotations into class that Ss can choose from.

4 Make note cards

> **Tip**
>
> ☐ Depending on your available class time and student level, you may want to have Ss start this activity in class and finish it as homework.
>
> ☐ If Ss need more help making effective note cards, collect their cards and give written feedback on them to the Ss.

- Read the instructions aloud and have Ss look back at the tips on page 16.
- Have Ss make their final notes on note cards or on paper that is folded or cut to postcard size. Tell Ss that they should have three note cards: one for the introduction, one for the body, and one for the conclusion.
- Point out the note card tip on page 19. If possible, use a note card yourself to show Ss how this technique can be useful when speaking.
- If Ss will be using PowerPoint for their presentations, bring their attention to the PowerPoint tip on the page.

5 Practice and present

- Read the instructions aloud.
- Remind Ss that the more they practice their presentation, the more confident they will feel when they are speaking.

- Explain the format and time limit for Ss' presentations (see tip below). Make sure Ss understand that they will be expected to use the language and presentation techniques they learned in Unit 1.

> **Tip**
>
> ☐ If time allows, have Ss form pairs or groups and take turns practicing their presentations in class. Suggest that Ss ask a classmate to time the length of their presentations and encourage them to make suggestions to help improve their classmates' presentations.
>
> ☐ Depending on class size, you will need to determine the best format (group or whole class) and time limit for Ss' presentations. The student presentations in the course are intended to be 3–5 minutes, but you can of course change the timing to suit your situation.

- If you plan to have Ss use the **Outline worksheet** and **Peer evaluation form** (pages 77 and 83), or if you plan to use the **Assessment form** (page 84) during Ss' presentations, be sure to make the appropriate number of copies before Ss begin their presentations.
- When Ss finish their presentations, have them complete the **Self-evaluation** on page 101 in the Student's Book.

Unit 1 Expansion activities

Pages 80–81

Guide: Ben

Activities	Unit 1 page no.
1 Introductions and conclusion	14
2 Openers and closers	15
3 Note card tips	16
4 Eye contact	17
5 PowerPoint tips	19
6 Unit goals checklist	8

1 Introductions and conclusions

▶ 1, 2, 3 Ss watch Patrick, Emma, and Jason from the **Focusing on language** lesson. Each speaker has added an introduction and a conclusion to their topic. Ss watch and identify what part of their introduction and conclusion each speaker forgets to include. Ss then watch Ben and check their answers.

1 Answers

Speaker	Introduction	Conclusion
Patrick	Opener	Signal phrase
Emma	Preview	Closer
Jason	Topic statement	Thanks

2 Openers and closers

▶ 4, 5, 6 Ss watch Patrick, Emma, and Jason from the **Focusing on language** lesson. Each speaker has added an opener and a closer to their topic. Ss watch and identify what type of opener and closer each speaker uses. Ss then watch Ben and check their answers.

2 Answers

Speaker	Opener	Closer
Patrick	a short story	a call to action
Emma	a question	statement about topic's importance
Jason	an interesting fact	pass the mike

3 Note card tips

▶ 7, 8 Ss read two body sections of Patrick's **Focusing on language** presentation and make a note card for each section using the note card tips on page 16. Ss then compare their note cards with Patrick's note cards on page 92. They then watch Patrick giving the same sections of his presentation using his note cards from page 92. While watching, Ss answer three questions that draw their attention to effective use of note cards. Ss then watch Ben and check their answers.

3B Answers

1 At chest level
2 Twice
3 No, he looks at the audience

4 Eye contact

▶ 9, 10, 11 Ss watch Patrick, Emma, and Jason from the **Focusing on language** lesson. However, in these three re-recorded versions, the speakers do not make effective use of eye contact. Each speaker does not follow at least one of the eye contact tips from page 17. Ss watch and try to identify which tip each speaker is not following. Ss then watch Sophie's presentation from the **Organizing ideas** lesson. Sophie displays effective eye contact. Ss then watch Ben and check their answers.

4 Answers

	Patrick	Emma	Jason	Sophie
Aim for 90 percent	X			
Look at someone for a sentence		X	X	✔
Use the read silently–look up– speak technique				
Hold note cards at chest level	X			✔
Don't be a lighthouse		X		✔
Think between people			X	✔

5 PowerPoint tips

▶ 12, 13 This activity focuses on the PowerPoint tips from page 19. Ss watch two versions of Patrick's presentation from the **Focusing on language** lesson. The first version is a re-recorded version in which Patrick does not use PowerPoint effectively. The second version is the original version: Patrick makes effective use of PowerPoint. While watching, Ss try to identify which version is good and what Patrick is doing wrong in the other version. Ss then watch Ben and check their answers.

5 Answers

Version 1
Bad: too much information on the slide; used complete sentences

Version 2
Good: used keywords and short phrases on slide

6 Unit goals checklist

Ss refer back to the unit goals and complete a checklist to assess how well they have achieved those goals.

2 A favorite place

Overview

All of the activities in the six lessons of Unit 2 guide Ss to the main goal of planning and giving a 3–5 minute presentation about a favorite place.

Lesson	Activities
Exploring the topic	Talking about different types of places and how often people go Completing a chart about Ss' favorite places
Focusing on language	Learning words to describe places Talking about activities people do in different places
Organizing ideas	Seeing how to brainstorm ideas and create an outline for a presentation about a favorite place Watching or listening to Ben's presentation about his favorite place – Venice Beach
Adding impact	Opener: general statement about people Closer: invitation
Developing presentation techniques	Gestures for description Body language: posture and hand position
Present yourself!	Brainstorming and organizing ideas for a presentation about a favorite place Giving a presentation to a group or the class

Exploring the topic

Pages 20–21

Vocabulary

cozy: a comfortable, pleasant, and inviting place, especially because it's small and warm

hang out: spend time in a place with someone, especially casually

historical: representing the past; very old

lively: having or showing a lot of energy; exciting, with a lot of people

spacious: having a lot of room, space

traditional: having an old-fashioned style

trendy: having the most recent or modern style; fashionable

window-shop: look at products in store windows without buying them

Frequency expressions
Expressions that show frequency include **once a week, twice a month, a few times a year**

1 Places

Lead-in

- Books closed. Tell Ss to think of a place where they like to spend time. Have them write down the place and three adjectives to describe it. Write an example on the board for Ss' reference. For example: Longview Park – big, open, beautiful.
- Have Ss share their places and adjectives in pairs. Then elicit adjectives from a few Ss and write them on the board.
- Tell Ss that in this unit, they will practice describing places where they like to spend time.

A

- Have Ss form pairs and tell them to open their books to page 20.
- Read the instructions and the words in the box aloud, with Ss repeating them.
- Explain any unfamiliar language.
- Have Ss describe the pictures in pairs.
- Walk around the classroom, helping Ss as necessary.

B

- Have Ss stay in their pairs from Exercise A.
- Read the instructions and the names of the places aloud. Explain any unfamiliar language. Make sure Ss understand the frequency expressions.
- Allow time for Ss to complete the chart.
- Model the next task. Ask: *How often do you go to an amusement park?* Have a S read the model language aloud.
- Walk around the classroom, helping Ss as necessary while they complete the activity.
- Take a class poll to find out the most popular places.

Tip

If there are Ss in the class who very rarely or never go to some of these places, have them change the right-hand column to *once or twice a year* or *never*.

C

- Have Ss stay in their pairs from Exercise B.
- Read the instructions aloud and have Ss tell their partner about other places where they spend time.
- Call on a few Ss to share their answers. Write the places on the board for Ss' reference.

2 Favorite places

A

- Tell Ss they will now have a chance to talk about some of their favorite places.

- Read the instructions aloud.
- Ask for volunteers to read the activities in the left column of the chart aloud. Explain any unfamiliar language.
- Point out the written example in the chart.
- Walk around the classroom, helping Ss as necessary while they complete the task.

B

- Have Ss stay in their pairs. Read the instructions aloud.
- Read the model conversation aloud with a S. Explain that Ss should have a similar conversation using their information from the chart in Exercise A.
- Remind Ss that they should take notes on their partners' answers because they will use that information when they do Exercise C.
- Walk around the classroom, helping Ss as necessary while they complete the task.

C

- Combine pairs to form groups of four.
- Point out the model language.
- Walk around the classroom, helping Ss as necessary while they complete the task.
- Ask for a few volunteers to share something interesting about a classmate.

Focusing on language

Pages 22–23

1 What's it like?

Vocabulary

bench: a long seat for two or more people, usually made of wood and used outside

narrow: having a small distance from one side to the other; opposite = **wide**

rug: a piece of thick cloth used to cover part of a floor

view: the scene that you can see from a particular place, for example, when looking out a window

A ◀)) ▶ 9

- Have Ss form pairs. Ask them to look at the pictures and guess what kind of places they are.
- Elicit answers from some pairs to see if the class agrees about the places.
- Read the instructions aloud.
- Encourage Ss to listen for keywords that will help them choose the correct pictures.
- Play the video or audio and have Ss mark their answers.

- Have Ss compare their answers in their pairs. Check answers by calling on individual Ss to describe the three pictures.
- Confirm answers by watching or listening again.

1A Answers

B 1 (Sophie)

C 3 (Emma)

D 2 (Jason)

B ◀)) ▶ 9

- Read the instructions aloud.
- Play the video or audio and have Ss mark their answers.
- Have Ss compare answers in pairs, then elicit answers from individual Ss.
- Confirm answers by watching or listening again.

1B Answers

Sophie:	a narrow path; lots of tall trees; so quiet and peaceful
Jason:	big green leather armchair; small and cozy; black-and-white photos
Emma:	bright and spacious; a little messy; a yellow rug

C

- Tell Ss that they are now going to play a guessing game to find out about nearby places.
- Read the instructions aloud and call on a S to read the written example aloud.
- Read the language in the box aloud and have Ss repeat it.
- Encourage Ss to use this language as they write their sentences on a piece of paper.

D

- Have Ss form groups of three or four.
- Read the instructions aloud and point out the model conversation.
- Walk around the classroom, helping Ss as necessary while Ss do the speaking task.
- Finish by playing the game with the whole class.

2 It's a great place to . . .

Vocabulary

enjoy some fresh air: go outdoors, often to somewhere pleasant – a park, in the country, etc.

get away from it all: take a break from regular, busy life and go somewhere to relax

watch people: the activity of looking at the people around you doing their normal activities

Usage note

homework vs. **housework**: Make sure Ss know the difference between homework (schoolwork) and housework (chores like cleaning, washing dishes, doing laundry).

A

- Read the instructions aloud.
- Read the list of activities aloud and have Ss repeat them. Explain any unfamiliar language.
- Call on a few Ss to share the activities they added. Write the activities on the board.

B ◀)) ▶ 10

- Read the instructions aloud.
- Play the video or audio and have Ss mark their answers.
- Have Ss compare answers in pairs. Then ask for volunteers to share their answers.

2B Answers

_J_	check email or Facebook
_S_	relax and think
_S_	enjoy some fresh air
_E_	get away from it all
_J_	watch people
_E_	listen to music
_J_	do homework
_S_	take pictures
_E_	play computer games

C

- Read the instructions aloud.
- Play the video or audio and have Ss write their answers on the lines.
- Have Ss compare answers in pairs. Then ask for volunteers to share their answers.

2C Possible answers

Sophie:	walk around the lake; feed the fish; take pictures of the lake
Jason:	do my homework
Emma:	play rock music; use keyboard to jam with the band

3 My favorite places

A

- Read the instructions aloud and point out the example in the chart.
- Walk around the classroom, helping Ss as necessary while they complete the chart.

B

- Have Ss form pairs.
- Read the instructions aloud.
- Read the model conversation aloud with a S. Explain that Ss should have a similar conversation using their information from the chart in Exercise A.
- Read the language in the box aloud and have Ss repeat it. Encourage them to use the language in this box and the one on page 22 for this activity.
- Walk around the classroom, helping Ss as necessary while they complete the activity.
- Finish by asking a few Ss to report back to the class about one of their partner's favorite places. To get Ss started, write on the board:
  My partner is _____ . One of his/her favorite places is _____ . It has _____ .

Organizing ideas

Pages 24–25

1 Ben's favorite place

Vocabulary

boardwalk: a path made of wooden boards on sand at the edge of a beach

bodysurf: surf (ride on waves) without a board

food stand: small shop selling various types food; also called **food stall**

open-air gym: a gym that is outside, not inside a building

remind: bring back a memory of something from the past

A

- Tell Ss to open their books to page 24, but have them cover Exercises B and C and page 25. Tell them to look only at the picture while you read the instructions and questions aloud.

Tip

The cover of the book also shows Venice Beach. You may want to have Ss look at this cover picture as well.

- Elicit several responses to the questions.
- Tell Ss they are going to find out about Ben's favorite place in this lesson of the unit.

1A Possible answers

Where: It's in North America / the US / California.

What: People are cycling/walking.

Why: He likes busy/lively places. He enjoys watching people / getting fresh air / being near the sea.

B

- Have Ss uncover their books and read the instructions aloud.
- Point out the brainstorming map on page 24 and the outline on page 25. Explain that Ben decided not to use a few of his brainstorming topics in his final presentation outline.
- Walk around the classroom, helping Ss as necessary while they complete the activity.
- Ask for volunteers to say the topics they checked.

1B Answers

General description of VB
What VB has
Interesting feature
When I go there
What I do there

2 Ben's presentation outline

Tip

Have Ss do this exercise in pairs, so they can help each other and share ideas.

A

- Read the instructions aloud. Explain that after Ben made his brainstorming map he thought of a few more details he wanted to include in his presentation.
- Explain any unfamiliar language.
- Walk around the classroom, helping Ss as necessary while they complete the activity.
- If Ss have been working individually, have them compare their answers in pairs.

B 🔊 ▶ 11

- Read the instructions aloud. Make sure Ss understand that they will see or hear Ben's whole presentation with the introduction and conclusion, but the outline is only for the body section.
- Play the video or audio and have Ss check their answers.
- Check answers by reading through the outline aloud and eliciting the missing information.

Tip

If Ss have trouble following Ben's presentation while watching or listening from only the outline, have them look at the full presentation on page 96 while they watch or listen again. Alternatively, if using the video, turn on the subtitles.

C

- Read the instructions aloud and have Ss form pairs.
- Tell Ss that you will ask some of them to tell the class what they found out about their partner.
- Walk around the classroom, helping Ss as necessary while they complete the activity.
- Ask for a few volunteers to share what they found out about their partner.

Adding impact

Pages 26–27

Note

In Units 2–6, each unit focuses on one type of opener and closer to begin and end a presentation. In each unit, it is the type of opener and closer that the speaker uses in the model presentation from the **Organizing ideas** lesson.

Lead-in

- Have Ss look at the **Introduction outline** at the top of the page.
- Remind Ss that in Unit 1, they learned about the parts that go into an introduction and conclusion.
- If necessary, have Ss quickly look back at pages 14–15 to jog their memories.

1 Opener: general statement about people

A 🔊 ► 12

- Read the explanation aloud. Clarify as necessary.
- Read the instructions aloud.
- Have Ss mark their answers, then compare with a partner.
- Play the video or audio and have Ss check their answers with their partner.
- Elicit the answer from Ss.

1A Answer

People have one type of place that is special to them.

B 🔊 ► 12

- Read the instructions aloud. Tell Ss that this time they need to listen more carefully for details.
- Play the video or audio and have Ss check their answers with their partner.
- Elicit the answers from Ss.
- If necessary, write the correct answers on the board for Ss' reference.

1B Answers

We all . . . I think everyone

2 Topic statement and preview

A

- Read the instructions aloud and have Ss complete the topic statement and preview.
- Ask Ss compare their answers with one or two classmates.

B 🔊 ► 13

- Read the instructions aloud.
- Play the video or audio and have Ss check their answers.
- If necessary, play the video or audio of Ben's whole introduction again while Ss look at the model presentation on page 96.

2B Answers

like to tell you . . . First, I'll describe . . . I'll tell you . . . talk about

Practice

- Have Ss form pairs. Read the instructions aloud.
- Read aloud the model language in the box. Have Ss repeat.
- Allow time for Ss to practice silently. Then ask them to present their opener to their partner. Point out the eye-contact reminder.
- Walk around the classroom, helping Ss as necessary while they complete the activity.
- Have Ss change partners and repeat. Tell Ss to try to use different examples in the box when they practice.

3 Concluding signal and review

A 🔊 ▶14

- Read the instructions aloud. Tell Ss to look at the conclusion outline.
- Have Ss individually or in pairs try to remember or guess the missing details in the outline.
- Play the video or audio and have Ss check their answers.
- Elicit answers from Ss and write them on the board.

B 🔊 ▶15

- Read the instructions aloud.
- Play the video or audio and have Ss check the answer.
- Elicit the answer from Ss.

4 Closer: invitation

A

- Read the explanation aloud. Clarify as necessary.
- Read the instructions aloud.
- Have Ss individually or in pairs try to remember or guess the missing words.

B 🔊 ▶15

- Read the instructions aloud.
- Play the video or audio and have Ss check their answers.
- Elicit the answers from Ss.

Practice

A

- Have Ss form pairs, Read the instructions aloud.
- Read aloud the model language in the box. Have Ss take turns using the language to practice Ben's conclusion.

B

- Read the instructions aloud and have Ss look at their notes for Exercise 3A on page 23.
- Tell Ss to imagine they have told their partner about one of their favorite places on page 23, and now they are ending their presentation.
- Allow Ss time to practice silently. Then ask them to present their closer to their partner.
- Walk around the classroom, helping Ss as necessary while they complete the activity.
- If Ss need more practice, have them change partners and repeat.
- Finish the lesson by emphasizing to Ss that a strong opener and closer really add a lot of impact to a presentation.

Developing presentation techniques

Pages 28–29

1 Gestures for descriptions

Lead-in

- Books closed. Tell Ss that you are going to communicate some words to them using only gestures. Tell them to watch you and write down the words they think you are trying to communicate.
- Stand in front of the class and clearly mime four or five descriptive adjectives similar to the ones on the page. For example: *long, tall, hot, straight*. Alternatively, write the words on cards. Then ask for volunteers to come to the front of the class, choose a card, and mime the word for the class.
- Have Ss compare the words they wrote with a partner.
- Tell Ss to open their books to page 28.

Vocabulary

browse: look at, just to see what is there; e.g., browse magazines in a shop

huge: very big; similar words = **enormous**, **gigantic**

oval: a flattened circle; shaped like an egg

tiny: very, very small

wavy: curving in shape; having a series of curves; not straight

windy: curving; not going in a straight line (pronounced *wine dee*)

A

- Read the instructions aloud.
- Model each of the six gestures for Ss.
- Walk around the classroom, helping Ss as necessary while they complete the activity.
- Have Ss compare their answers in pairs.
- Elicit answers from volunteers and correct as necessary.

1A Answers

1	C	3	A	5	E
2	F	4	B	6	D

B

- Read the instructions aloud.
- Have Ss practice the gestures in pairs. Remind them to make the gestures slowly and clearly and also to make eye contact with their partner when they are speaking.
- Ask a few volunteers to stand up and demonstrate for the class.

Practice

A

- Read the instructions aloud.
- Walk around the classroom, helping Ss as necessary while they complete the activity. Make sure that Ss write their own sentence for number 5.
- Have Ss practice on their own presenting their sentences with gestures.

B

- Read the instructions aloud.
- Have Ss form pairs or small groups to do the guessing game.
- Ask for a few volunteers to demonstrate for the class.

Tip

Model the presentation tip on page 29 by giving a brief description of a place (e.g., the school library, your own home, a city park, a nearby café) using slightly exaggerated gestures.

2 Body language: posture and hand position

A

- Read the explanation and instructions aloud. Clarify as appropriate.
- Walk around the classroom, helping Ss as necessary while they complete the activity.
- Have Ss compare their answers in pairs.
- Elicit answers from volunteers and make sure the class agrees about the Dos and Don'ts.

1A Answers

A	Do	D	Do
B	Don't	E	Don't
C	Don't	F	Do

B

- Read the instructions aloud.
- Model each of the six posture and hand positions yourself, slightly exaggerating them.
- Walk around the classroom, helping Ss as necessary while they complete the activity.
- Have Ss compare their answers in pairs.
- Elicit answers from volunteers and correct as necessary.

1B Answers

1	B	4	E
2	D	5	C
3	F (A also possible)	6	A (F also possible)

Practice

A

- Read the instructions aloud.
- Walk around the classroom, helping Ss as necessary while they complete the activity.
- Have Ss compare their answers in pairs.
- Elicit answers from volunteers and correct as necessary.

A Answers

tall; narrow; long; large oval; big, thick

B

- Read the instructions aloud.
- Allow Ss time to practice on their own.
- Have Ss form pairs and take turns presenting Sam's Books. Remind Ss to stand up and use gestures and also to follow the body language tips.
- Walk around the classroom, helping Ss as necessary while they complete the activity.
- Ask for a few volunteers to demonstrate for the class.
- Finish the activity by telling Ss that they are now ready to plan and give their own presentation about a favorite place.

Present yourself!

Pages 30–31

1 Brainstorm

- Read the assignment and instructions aloud.
- As a reminder, have the Ss look again at Ben's brainstorming map on page 24.
- Give Ss enough time to partially or fully complete their brainstorming maps. Encourage Ss to include information and details they think their classmates will find interesting
- Walk around the classroom, helping Ss as necessary while they complete the activity.

2 Organize

- Read the instructions aloud.
- Have Ss look again at Ben's outline on page 25, as necessary.
- Point out that the Ss can add their own topics wherever they think they fit best into their outline.
- Give Ss time to think of a presentation title and complete the outline.
- Walk around the classroom, helping Ss as necessary while they complete the activity.

Tip

If Ss need more help organizing their outlines, collect the outlines and give written feedback on them to the Ss.

3 Add impact

- Tell Ss that the above outline is for the body of their presentation. It's time to think about the introduction and conclusion to make the presentation complete and balanced.
- Read the instructions aloud.

- Elicit or remind Ss what type of opener and closer Ben used in his presentation (**Answers**: general statement, invitation). If necessary, have Ss look back at pages 26–27 and the model presentation on page 96.
- Give Ss enough time to complete their notes for the introduction and conclusion or ask Ss to complete them at home.

Tip

To reinforce Ss' learning about introductions and conclusions:

- ☐ Have Ss look at Ben's model presentation on page 96. Ask them to underline the key language he uses for his opener, topic statement, preview, conclusion signal phrase, review, and closer.
- ☐ Remind Ss of the type of opener and closer that Sophie uses in her model presentation about her friend Kate (quotation). Tell Ss that they can use a quote or proverb about places to end their presentations if they prefer.

4 Make note cards

Tip

- ☐ Depending on your available class time and student level, you may want to have Ss start this activity in class and finish it as homework.
- ☐ If Ss need more help making effective note cards, collect their cards and give written feedback on them to the Ss.

- Read the instructions aloud and have Ss look back at the tips on page 16.
- Have Ss make their final notes on note cards or, if that is not possible, on paper that is folded or cut to postcard size. Tell Ss that they should have three note cards: one for the introduction, one for the body, and one for the conclusion.
- Point out the note card tip on page 31 and read it aloud. If possible, use a note card yourself to show the Ss how this technique can be useful when speaking.
- If Ss will be using PowerPoint for their presentations, point out the PowerPoint tips on the page and read them aloud.

5 Practice and present

- Read the instructions aloud.
- Remind Ss that the more they practice their presentation, the more confident they will feel when they are speaking.
- Explain the format and time limit for Ss' presentations (see tip below). Make sure Ss understand that they will be expected to use the language and presentation techniques they learned in Unit 2.

Tip

- ☐ If time allows, have Ss form pairs or groups and take turns practicing their presentations in class. Suggest that Ss ask a classmate to time the length of their presentations and encourage them to make suggestions to help improve their classmates' presentations.

- ☐ Although PowerPoint is not necessary for this presentation, if time and classroom technology permit, ask the Ss to each use two or three photos of their favorite place on slides while they are speaking. Alternatively, they could print photos of their favorite place from the Internet. Remind Ss to make sure their pictures are big enough for everyone to see.

- ☐ Depending on class size, you will need to determine the best format (group or whole class) and time limit for Ss' presentations. The student presentations in the course are intended to be 3–5 minutes, but you can of course change the timing to suit your situation.

- If you plan to have Ss use the **Outline worksheet** and **Peer evaluation form** (pages 78 and 83), or if you plan to use the **Assessment form** (page 84) during Ss' presentations, be sure to make the appropriate number of copies before Ss begin their presentations.
- When Ss finish their presentations, have them complete the **Self-evaluation** on page 102 in the Student's Book.

Unit 2 Expansion activities
Pages 82–83

Guide: Grace

Activity	Unit 2 page no.
1 Openers and closers	26–27
2 Gestures for descriptions	28
3 Body language and posture	29
4 PowerPoint tips	31
5 Unit goals checklist	20

1 Openers and closers

▶ 14, 15, 16 Ss watch Patrick, Emma, and Jason from the **Focusing on language** lesson. Each speaker has added an introduction and a conclusion to their topic. Ss watch and identify the type of opener and closer each speaker uses. Ss then watch Grace and check their answers.

1 Answers

Speaker	Opener	Closer
Sophie	a question	a statement about the topic's importance
Jason	an interesting fact	a recommendation or invitation
Emma	a quotation or proverb	pass the mike

2 Gestures for descriptions

▶ 17, 18, 19 Ss read a section of Emma's presentation from the **Focusing on language** lesson and underline the descriptive adjectives that can be emphasized with gestures. Ss then watch Emma and check their answers. They then watch a section of Ben's model presentation about Venice Beach and write the descriptive adjectives that he emphasizes with gestures. Ss then watch Grace and check their answers.

Answers

2A Emma: There's a tall window on one wall, so I have a great view of the park across the street. On the other walls, there are a few posters of my favorite bands, and on the floor, I have a yellow rug. It's not so big, maybe about <u>this long</u>. Actually, you can't see it very often because it's usually covered with a <u>huge</u> pile of my clothes, books, and stuff that comes up to <u>about here</u>!

2B Ben: wide; next to (the beach); small, narrow

3 Body language and posture

▶ 20, 21, 22 In Exercise A, Ss watch Sophie and Jason from the **Focusing on language** lesson. However, in these re-recorded versions, the speakers don't make effective use of body language. Each speaker does *not* follow at least one of the Dos and Don'ts from page 29. Ss watch and try to identify the tips the speakers do not follow. In Exercise B, Ss watch Ben giving part of his presentation and identify the tips that he follows. Ben makes very effective use of body language and follows all of the body language tips. In Exercise C, Ss watch Grace and check their answers.

3 Answers

	Sophie	Jason	Ben
Do stand straight but relaxed with your feet 30 to 45 centimeters apart	X		✔
Don't lean against a desk or table for support when speaking		X	✔
Don't cross your arms in front of your chest to show your confidence		X	✔
Do smile naturally to show you are comfortable with your message	X		✔
Don't touch your face or hair, or put your hands in your pockets	X	X	✔
Do keep your hands by your side or at waist level with elbows loose when not gesturing	X	X	✔

4 PowerPoint tips

▶ 23, 24 This activity focuses on the PowerPoint tips from page 31. Ss watch two versions of Ben's model presentation. The first version is a re-recorded version in which Ben does not use PowerPoint effectively. The second version is the original version: Ben makes effective use of PowerPoint. While watching, Ss try to identify which version is good and what Ben is doing wrong in the other version. Ss then watch Grace and check their answers.

4 Answers

Version 1
Bad: stands in front of the screen; turns his back to the audience

Version 2
Good: stood to one side of the screen; faced the audience

5 Unit goals checklist

Ss refer back to the unit goals and complete a checklist to assess how well they have achieved those goals.

3 A prized possession

Overview

All of the activities in the six lessons of Unit 3 guide Ss to the main goal of planning and giving a 3–5 minute presentation about a prized possession.

Lesson	Activities
Exploring the topic	Talking about possessions and what makes them important to people Conducting a survey about classmates' possessions
Focusing on language	Describing prized possessions Explaining the history and use of a possession
Organizing ideas	Seeing how to brainstorm ideas and create an outline for a presentation about a prized possession Watching or listening to Grace's presentation about her prized pencil case
Adding impact	Opener: question Closer: emphasize why something is special
Developing presentation techniques	Showing an object to an audience Using show-and-tell expressions to point out the features of an object
Present yourself!	Brainstorming and organizing ideas for a presentation about a prized possession Giving a presentation about a prized possession to a group or the class

Exploring the topic

Pages 32–33

Vocabulary

achievement: something you did or got after planning a lot and working hard

bring back memories: make you think about events or people from the past

meaningful: having importance or value

prized possession: an object that is very important or valuable to you

save time: make a job or task easier and faster

scented: having a pleasant smell

souvenir: something to help you remember a holiday or special event

trophy: a prize given to the winner of a competition, for example, a large silver cup or bowl

1 People and their possessions

Lead-in

Books closed. Explain or elicit the meaning of *prized possession*. Ask Ss to name some of their own important or prized possessions. Tell them to think about why the possessions are important and elicit a few responses from the class, e.g., *It cost a lot of money. I've had it for a long time. It was a gift from my parents.* You could also give an example of one of your own prized possessions and say why it's important to you.

A

- Tell Ss to open their books to page 32.
- Have Ss look at the pictures while you read the instructions aloud.
- Read the names of the possessions aloud.
- Explain any unfamiliar vocabulary
- Point out the categories in the chart and the example.
- Have Ss complete the chart. Make sure Ss understand that there are no right or wrong answers. They can decide which possession goes in each category.
- Walk around the classroom, helping Ss as necessary.

B

- Have Ss form pairs.
- Read the instructions aloud.
- Ask two Ss to read the model conversation aloud. Explain that Ss should have a similar conversation using their information from the chart.
- Walk around the classroom, helping pairs as necessary while they share their ideas.
- Elicit a few possessions for each category in the chart in Exercise A.

2 Possessions survey

> **Vocabulary**
>
> **award**: a gift of money or a prize to someone following an official decision

A

- Tell Ss that they will now have a chance to talk about some of their important possessions.
- Read the instructions aloud.
- Call on Ss to read the phrases in the left column of the chart aloud. Explain any unfamiliar language.
- Point out the model language and the written example in the chart.
- Have Ss stand and interview their classmates. Tell Ss to ask each question to a different classmate and write their classmates' answers in the chart.
- Walk around the classroom, helping Ss as necessary.

B

- Read the instructions aloud.
- Point out the model language.
- Ask for a few volunteers to share information about their classmates' possessions.

3 My prized possessions

A

- Read the instructions aloud.
- Point out the written example in the chart.
- Give Ss time to complete the chart individually.
- Walk around the classroom, helping Ss as necessary.

B

- Have Ss form pairs.
- Read the instructions aloud.
- Point out the model language.
- When Ss have finished, ask for volunteers to tell the class about one of their prized possessions.

Focusing on language

Pages 34–35

1 What does it look like?

> **Vocabulary**
>
> **condition**: the state that something is in, for example, new, old, broken
>
> **faded**: being a paler color than when new
>
> **inch**: equal to 2.54 centimeters
>
> **material**: the substance (metal, glass, etc.) that an object is made of
>
> **patch**: a piece of cloth used to cover a hole on clothing
>
> **pattern**: a regular arrangement of lines, shapes, designs, or colors
>
> **rough**: not smooth or even
>
> **smooth**: having an even surface
>
> **swirls**: a design with lines that twist around in a circle from the middle
>
> **texture**: the way something feels when you touch it

A ◀◧ ▶ 16

- Read the instructions aloud.
- Play the video or audio and have Ss mark their answers.
- Have Ss compare answers in pairs. Then elicit answers from individual Ss.

1A Answers

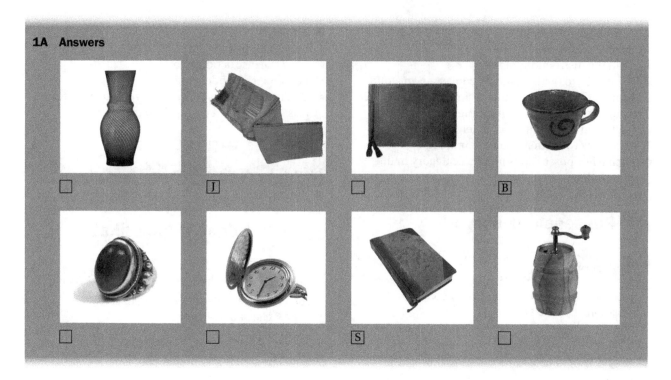

☐   J   ☐   B

☐   ☐   S   ☐

B 🔊 ▶ 16

Tip

Before Ss listen a second time, ask them to try to remember any of the words that Jason, Sophie, and Ben used to describe their possessions. Ss can then confirm their answers with the second listening.

- Read the instructions aloud.
- Play the video or audio and have Ss mark their answers.
- Have Ss compare answers in pairs. Then elicit answers from individual Ss.
- Confirm any answers Ss don't know or aren't sure about by playing the video or audio.

1B Answers

Jason	Sophie	Ben
original dark	blue silk cloth	rough
square	smooth	cool, gray, round
big hole	it's brown leather	round, thick

C

Lead-in

Books closed. Write the categories from the chart in Exercise B on the board (size, shape, texture, condition, pattern, material). Tell Ss that in this lesson, they are going to practice describing possessions. Describe one of your possessions (e.g., a piece of clothing, jewelry, bag), using an adjective from each of the categories on the board and have Ss guess what the possession is. When Ss have guessed your possession, elicit the adjectives you used to describe the possession and write them next to the appropriate categories on the board.

- Read the instructions aloud.
- Point out the examples in the box. Explain any unfamiliar vocabulary.
- Have Ss complete the chart on their own, then compare their answers in pairs.
- Elicit answers from individual Ss. Write the Ss' own words on the board and make sure the class understands the meanings of the new words.

D

- Have Ss form new pairs.
- Read the instructions aloud.
- Read the language in the box aloud and have Ss repeat it. Ask Ss to use this language when they do the activity.
- Call on two Ss to read the model conversation aloud.
- Walk around the classroom, helping Ss as necessary while they play the guessing game.
- Ask a few volunteers to describe their possession aloud while the whole class guesses.

2 Here's the history

A 🔊 ▶ 17

- Read the instructions aloud.
- Play the video or audio and have Ss mark their answers.
- Have Ss compare answers in pairs. Then elicit answers from individual Ss.

2A Answers

		Where I got it	How long I've had it	How I use it
1	Jason	at an outlet store	for seven years	when I relax with friends
2	Sophie	from my parents	since high school	to write thoughts
3	Ben	in Italy	since last summer	to drink coffee

B ◀)) ▶ 17

Tip

Before Ss listen a second time, ask them to try to remember what Jason, Sophie, and Ben said about their possessions by writing in their guesses. Ss can then confirm their answers with the second listening.

- Read the instructions aloud.
- Play the video or audio and have Ss complete the sentences on the lines.
- Have Ss compare answers in pairs. Then elicit answers from individual Ss.
- Confirm any unknown or unsure answers by playing the video or audio again.

C

- Read the instructions aloud.
- Point out the example in the chart.
- Allow time for Ss to complete the chart individually.
- Walk around the classroom, helping Ss as necessary.

D

- Have Ss form pairs.
- Read the instructions aloud.
- Read the language in the box aloud and have Ss repeat it. Ask Ss to use this language when they do the activity.
- Call on two Ss to read the model conversation aloud.
- Walk around the classroom, helping Ss as necessary while they play the guessing game.
- Ask a few volunteers to describe their possession's history and its use aloud.

Usage note

for vs. **since**: The difference in usage between *for* and *since* can be confusing for Ss but is actually simple. *For* is followed by a period of time, e.g., *for two hours / three days / a month / five years*; *since* is followed by a specific date, time or period of history, e.g., *since last year / 2012 / I was 10 years old / high school*

Organizing ideas

Pages 36–37

Vocabulary

broken: damaged or no longer able to work

feature: an important or special part of something

make something by hand: create something yourself, not by using a machine

1 Grace's prized possession

A

- Tell Ss to open their books to page 36, but have them cover Exercises B and C and page 37.
- Tell Ss to look only at the picture while you read the instructions and questions aloud.
- Elicit several responses to the questions.
- Tell Ss they are going to find out why this is Grace's prized possession in this lesson.

B

- Have Ss uncover their books and read the instructions aloud.
- Point out the brainstorming map on page 36 and the outline on page 37. Explain that Grace decided not to use a few of her brainstorming topics in her final presentation outline.
- Walk around the classroom, helping Ss as necessary while they complete the activity.
- Ask for volunteers to say the topics they checked.

1B Answers

Description
Condition
History: how and when I got it
How I use it now

2 Grace's presentation outline

Tip

Have Ss do this exercise in pairs, so they can help each other and share ideas.

A

- Read the instructions aloud. Explain that after Grace made her brainstorming map she thought of a few more details she wanted to include in her presentation.
- Explain any unfamiliar language.

- Walk around the classroom, helping Ss as necessary while they complete the activity.
- If Ss have been working individually, have them compare their answers in pairs.

B 🔊 ▶ 18
- Read the instructions aloud. Make sure Ss understand that they will see or hear Grace's whole presentation with the introduction and conclusion, but the outline is only for the body section.
- Play the video or audio and have Ss check their answers.
- Check answers by reading the outline aloud and eliciting the missing information.

2B Answers

A Description: in the middle: narrow row of triangles; made of thick cotton cloth with zipper at top

B Condition: colors used to be much brighter

C History: how and when I got it: gift from Grannie when I started elem. school; Grannie said it'll help me get good grades

D How I use it now: have around 20 pens or pencils in it; use pens, pencils to brainstorm, write notes

Tip

If Ss have trouble understanding Grace's presentation while watching or listening from only the outline, have them look at the full presentation on page 97 while they watch or listen again. Alternatively, if using the video, turn on the subtitles.

C
- Read the instructions aloud and have Ss form pairs.
- Tell Ss that you will ask some of them to tell the class what they found out about their partner.
- Walk around the classroom, helping Ss as necessary while they complete the activity.
- Ask for a few volunteers to share what they found out about their partner.

Adding impact

Pages 38–39

Note

In Units 2–6, each unit focuses on one type of opener and closer to begin and end a presentation. In these units, it is the type of opener and closer that the speaker uses in their model presentation from the **Organizing ideas** lesson.

1 Opener: question

Lead-in
- Remind Ss that in Units 1 and 2, they learned about two different ways to open and close a presentation. In this unit, they are going to learn about another way they can begin and end a presentation.
- Read the explanation aloud.
- Have Ss look at the introduction outline at the top of the page.

A
- Read the instructions aloud.
- If necessary, have Ss look back at pages 36–37 to jog their memories.
- Elicit answers from Ss about Grace's possible question.
- Have Ss write other possible questions Grace could ask to begin her presentation.
- Have Ss share their ideas in pairs. Then elicit answers from Ss and write Ss' questions on the board.

1A Possible answers

Any of the questions in Exercise C on page 37 could be used as an opener.

B 🔊 ▶ 19
- Tell Ss they will now compare their opening questions with Grace's.
- Read the instructions aloud.
- Play the video or audio and have Ss complete Grace's opener.
- Have Ss check their answers with their partner.

1B Answer

you would be very sad to lose

2 Topic statement and preview

A
- Read the instructions aloud.
- Tell Ss to write their answers.
- Have Ss compare their answers with one or two classmates.

B 🔊 ▶ 20
- Read the instructions aloud.
- Play the video or audio and have Ss check their answers.
- Make any necessary corrections to the answers on the board.

- If necessary, play the video or audio of Grace's whole introduction again while Ss look at the model presentation on page 97.

2B Answers

share . . . point out . . . tell you a little . . . talk about

Practice

- Have Ss form pairs. Read the instructions aloud.
- Read aloud the model language in the box. Have Ss repeat.
- Make sure Ss understand that they should use their own questions from Exercise 1A for this activity.
- Allow time for Ss to practice silently. Then ask them to present their opener to their partner. Point out the body language reminder.
- Walk around the classroom, helping Ss as necessary while they complete the activity.
- If Ss need more practice, have them change partners and repeat.

3 Concluding signal and review

A ◄)) ► 21
- Read the explanation at the top of the page aloud.
- Read the instructions aloud. Then have Ss look at the Conclusion outline box.
- Have Ss individually or in pairs try to remember or guess the correct signal phrase.
- Play the video or audio and have Ss check their answers.
- Elicit the answer from Ss and write it on the board.

3A Answer

In conclusion

B ◄)) ► 21
- Read the instructions aloud.
- Have Ss individually or in pairs try to remember or guess the features from Grace's review.
- Play the video or audio and have Ss mark their answers.
- Elicit answers from Ss.

3B Answers

☑ It's useful   ☑ It's old   ☐ It's expensive
☐ It's colorful   ☑ It's made of cloth

4 Closer: emphasize why something is special

A
- Read the explanation aloud.
- Have Ss individually or in pairs try to remember or guess the missing words.
- Elicit answers from Ss and write them on the board.

B ◄)) ► 22
- Read the instructions aloud.
- Play the video or audio and have Ss write in their answers.
- Elicit answers from Ss.

4B Answers

It's not because . . . It's because . . . It's because . . . Most of all

Phrase repeated three times: *It's because*

Practice

A
- Have Ss form pairs. Read the instructions aloud.
- Read aloud the model language in the box. Have Ss repeat.
- Walk around the classroom, helping Ss as necessary while they complete the activity.

B
- Read the instructions aloud and have Ss look at their notes for Exercise 3A on page 33.
- Tell Ss to imagine that they have told their partner about one of their prized possessions on page 33, and now they want to end their presentation by emphasizing why it is special.
- Allow time for Ss to practice silently. Then ask them to present their closer to their partner.
- Walk around the classroom, helping Ss as necessary while they complete the activity.
- If Ss need more practice, have them change partners and repeat.
- Finish the lesson by emphasizing to Ss that a strong opener and closer really add a lot of impact to a presentation.

Developing presentation techniques

Pages 40–41

Vocabulary

torn: damaged by being pulled apart from something else, for example, a *torn short*

wave around: move something around quickly in all directions while holding it.

Tip

Before you begin this lesson, select an item that you can use to demonstrate show-and-tell. Be sure to select something that you can easily hold up and that Ss will be able to see.

1 Showing a possession

Lead-in

- Books closed. Tell Ss that you are going to show them one of your possessions and tell them about it.
- Hold up the possession and describe its physical features, modeling the show-and-tell tips and expressions from pages 40–41.
- When you finish, try to elicit some of the tips and show-and-tell expressions you used. Tell Ss that they are going to practice showing a possession clearly to an audience.
- Have Ss open their books to page 40.
- Read the explanation at the top of the page aloud.

A

- Read the instructions aloud.
- Have Ss form pairs to share their ideas.
- Walk around the classroom, helping Ss as necessary while they complete the activity.
- Elicit answers from volunteers and correct as necessary.

1A   Possible answers *(left to right, top to bottom)*

1   The object and its features are not big enough for the audience to see clearly.

2   He is not showing all the parts of the object: front, back, inside, etc.

3   He is holding the object in front of his face.

4   The audience cannot see the object clearly. Books are blocking the audience's view.

5   The object is too small to be seen clearly. He is not holding the object so everyone can see it.

B

- Read the instructions aloud, along with the tips in the box.
- Walk around the classroom, helping Ss as necessary while they mark their answers.
- Have Ss form pairs to compare their answers.
- Elicit answers and correct as necessary.

1B   Possible answers *(left to right, top to bottom)*

Tip 1:   Picture 1 or Picture 5

Tip 2:   Picture 2

Tip 3:   Picture 3

Tip 4:   Picture 1 or Picture 5

Tip 5:   Picture 4

Practice

- Tell Ss that now they will have a chance to practice showing a possession.
- Read the instructions aloud.
- Tell Ss to look at the information in the box.
- Have Ss form pairs to complete the activity.
- Read aloud the model language.
- Walk around the classroom, helping Ss as necessary while they complete the activity.
- If Ss need more practice, have them change partners and repeat.
- Ask for a few volunteers to demonstrate for the class.

Tip

For further practice, have Ss change the information in the box at the bottom of page 40 to match their own photo album or an imaginary notebook. Alternatively, have Ss exchange notebooks with classmates and repeat the activity using the new notebooks.

2 Show-and-tell expressions

- Read the explanation at the top of the page aloud.
- Read aloud the instruction and expressions in the box.
- Walk around the classroom, helping Ss as necessary while they mark their answers.
- Have Ss compare their answers in pairs.
- Elicit answers and correct as necessary.

2A   Answers *(left to right, top to bottom)*

A   Picture 2

B   Picture 5

C   Picture 3

D   Picture 4

E   Picture 1

A

- Read the instructions aloud.
- Give Ss time to choose an object they have with them and make notes in the box.
- Remind Ss to write only notes, not complete sentences, in the box.
- Walk around the classroom, helping Ss as necessary while they complete the activity.

B

- Read the instructions aloud.
- Have pairs from Exercise 2B join together to form groups of four or six Ss.
- Read the expressions from the box aloud.
- Make sure Ss understand that for this activity they should change the language in the box to fit the possession they are describing.
- Allow time for Ss to practice with their object on their own.
- Remind Ss to use the show-and-tell tips from page 40 when they show their object.
- Walk around the classroom, helping Ss as necessary while they complete the activity.
- Ask for a few volunteers to demonstrate for the class.
- When Ss finish, tell them that they are now ready to begin planning their own presentations about a prized possession.

Tip

For more realistic presentation practice, have Ss stand up when it is their turn to show their possession to their group members. Remind Ss of the eye contact and body language tips from Units 1 and 2.

Present yourself!

Pages 42–43

1 Brainstorm

- Read the assignment and instructions aloud.
- As a reminder, have the Ss look again at Grace's brainstorming map on page 36.
- Give Ss enough time to partially or fully complete their brainstorming maps. Encourage Ss to include information and details they think their classmates will find interesting.
- Walk around the classroom, helping Ss as necessary while they complete the activity.

2 Organize

- Read the instructions aloud.
- Have Ss look again at Grace's outline on page 37, as necessary.
- Point out that the Ss can add their own topics wherever they think they fit best into their outline.
- Give Ss time to think of a presentation title and complete the outline.
- Walk around the classroom, helping Ss as necessary while they complete the activity.

Tip

If Ss need more help organizing their outlines, collect the outlines and give written feedback on them to the Ss.

3 Add impact

- Tell Ss that the above outline is for the body of their presentation. It's time to think about the introduction and conclusion to make the presentation complete and balanced.
- Read the instructions aloud.
- Elicit or remind Ss what type of opener and closer Grace used in her presentation. (**Answers:** question; emphasize why something is special). If necessary, have Ss look back at pages 38 and 39 and the model presentation on page 97.
- Give Ss enough time to complete their notes for the introduction and conclusion or ask Ss to complete them at home.

Tip

To reinforce Ss' learning about introductions and conclusions:

☐ Have Ss look at the model presentation on page 97. Ask them to underline the key language Grace uses for her opener, topic statement, preview, conclusion signal phrase, review, and closer.

☐ Remind Ss of the type of openers and closers that Sophie and Ben used in their model presentations in Units 1 and 2. Tell Ss that if they don't want to use the opener and closer from this unit, they can use the ones from Units 1 or 2.

4 Make note cards

Tip

- ☐ Depending on your available class time and student level, you may want to have Ss start this activity in class and finish it as homework.
- ☐ If Ss need more help making effective note cards, collect their cards and give written feedback on them to the Ss.

- Read the instructions aloud and have Ss look back at the tips on page 16.
- Have Ss make their final notes on note cards or, if that is not possible, on paper that is folded or cut to postcard size. Tell Ss that they should have three note cards: one for the introduction, one for the body, and one for the conclusion.
- Point out the note card tip on page 43 and read it aloud. If possible, use a note card yourself to show the Ss how this technique can be useful when speaking.
- If Ss will be using PowerPoint for their presentations, point out the PowerPoint tip on page 43 and read it aloud.

5 Practice and present

- Read the instructions aloud.
- Remind Ss that the more they practice their presentation, the more confident they will feel when they are speaking.
- Explain the format and time limit for Ss' presentations. Make sure Ss understand that they will be expected to use the language and presentation techniques they learned in Unit 3.

Tip

- ☐ If time allows, have Ss form pairs or groups and take turns practicing their presentations in class. Suggest that Ss ask a classmate to time the length of their presentations, and encourage them to make suggestions to help improve their classmates' presentations.
- ☐ Although PowerPoint is not necessary for this presentation, if time and classroom technology permit, ask Ss each to use two to three close-up photos of their possession on slides while they are speaking. Alternatively, they could print photos of specific features of their object. Remind Ss to make sure their pictures are big enough for everyone to see.
- ☐ Depending on class size, you will need to determine the best format (group or whole class) and time limit for Ss' presentations. The student presentations in the course are intended to be 3–5 minutes, but please feel free to change the timing to suit your situation.

- If you plan to have Ss use the **Outline worksheet** and **Peer evaluation form** (pages 79 and 83), or if you plan to use the **Assessment form** (page 84) during Ss' presentations, be sure to make the appropriate number of copies before Ss begin their presentations.
- When Ss finish their presentations, have them complete the **Self-evaluation** on page 103 in the Student's Book.

Unit 3 Expansion activities

Pages 84–85

Guide: Patrick

Activity	Unit 3 page no.
1 Openers and closers	38–39
2 Show-and-tell tips	40
3 Show-and-tell expressions	41
4 Note card tips	43
5 PowerPoint tips	43
6 Unit goals checklist	32

1 Openers and closers

▶ 25, 26, 27 Ss watch Jason, Sophie, and Ben from the **Focusing on language** lesson. Each speaker has added an introduction and a conclusion to their topic. Ss watch and identify the type of opener and closer each speaker uses. Ss then watch Patrick and check their answers.

> **1 Answers**
>
> | Speaker | Opener | Closer |
> |---|---|---|
> | Jason | mystery list | call to action |
> | Sophie | question | statement about importance of her possession |
> | Ben | general statement | thought about the future |

2 Show-and-tell tips

▶ 28, 29 Ss review the show-and-tell tips from page 40, then watch two versions of a section from Grace's presentation about her pencil case. Ss make notes as they watch the two versions, noticing what Grace does badly and well. The first version is a re-recorded version in which she doesn't show her possession effectively because she doesn't follow some of the tips. The second version is the original version: Grace follows the tips. Ss then watch Patrick and check their answers.

> **2 Answers**
>
> **Version 1**
> Bad: waved the case around; didn't show its features clearly; photo showing features was too small
>
> **Version 2**
> Good: held the case so everyone could see; highlighted its special features; photo of features large enough for all to see

3 Show-and-tell expressions

▶ 30 Ss read a section of Grace's presentation with key show-and-tell expressions closed out. Ss try to supply the correct expressions. Ss then watch Grace and check their answers. Ss then watch Patrick and confirm their answers.

> **3 Answers**
>
> all see it clearly . . . you look closely . . . in the middle . . . you can see clearly . . . this end . . . near the top

4 Note card tips

Ss review the note card tip about writing simple stage directions from the **Present yourself!** lesson on page 43. Ss then make a note card with stage directions of the section of Grace' presentation in Exercise 3 on page 84. Finally, Ss compare their note card to Grace's note card on page 93.

> **4 Answers**
>
> See the note card on page 93, which shows Grace's note card with stage directions on the left in red. The note card also follows other note card tips: use of colors, caps, and different fonts to highlight key points; use of phrases and keywords, not full sentences

5 PowerPoint tips

▶ 31, 32 This activity focuses on the PowerPoint tip from page 43. In Exercise A, Ss read a section of Sophie's presentation from the **Focusing on language** lesson and mark each place they think Sophie shows a picture. Ss then watch Sophie and check their answers. In Exercise B, Ss make notes in a chart to evaluate how effectively Sophie uses pictures of her possession (her journal). In Exercise C, Ss watch Patrick and check their answers.

> **5A Answers**
>
> **PICTURE 1** *I'd like to share this very special possession with you. As you can see, it's pretty small, so it fits easily into my bag. However, it's also around an inch thick because it has 250 pages. I love the cover. Can you see?* **PICTURE 2** *It's made of blue silk cloth, which feels really smooth. And it has a beautiful oriental design with bamboo trees and pagodas. Here,* **PICTURE 3** *on the edge and on the corners, it's brown leather. It's difficult to see, but here on the leather there are butterflies.*

5B   Answers

Pictures	Picture of what?	Large and clear?	Helpful?
1	full diary cover	☺ ☹	☺ ☹
2	closeup of cover showing silk design	☺ ☹	☺ ☹
3	closeup of corner showing leather butterflies	☺ ☹	☺ ☹

6   Unit goals checklist

Ss refer back to the unit goals on page 32 and complete a checklist to assess how well they have achieved those goals.

4 A memorable experience

Overview

All of the activities in the six lessons of this unit guide Ss to the main goal of planning and giving a 3–5 minute presentation about a memorable experience.

Lesson	Activities
Exploring the topic	Relating experiences and feelings associated with them Interviewing classmates about their experiences and feelings
Focusing on language	Setting the scene for an experience Using time expressions to describe an experience
Organizing ideas	Seeing how to brainstorm ideas and create an outline for a presentation about a memorable experience Watching or listening to Patrick's presentation about his memorable experience: scuba diving
Adding impact	Opener: mystery list Closer: "pass the mike"
Developing presentation techniques	Using your voice: volume, clear speech, avoiding fillers Using stress to emphasize intensifiers
Present yourself!	Brainstorming and organizing ideas for a presentation about a memorable experience Giving a presentation about a memorable experience to a group or class

Exploring the topic

Pages 44–45

Vocabulary

embarrassing: causing you to feel stupid or ashamed

exhausting: causing you to feel very tired

frustrating: causing you to feel unhappy because of a lack of success or not being able to meet goals

memorable: something that is likely to be remembered for a long time after it happened

robbed: when your money or things are taken from you illegally

scary: causing you to feel afraid

terrifying: causing you to feel very afraid

thrilled: feeling very pleased and excited

Usage note

bored vs. **boring**: Ss often confuse the -ed and -ing endings of participial adjectives. If necessary, spend a little time clarifying the difference. Explain that the cause of a feeling has an -ing ending. For example, *The movie was frightening*. (The movie was the cause of the feeling). Explain that the receiver of a feeling has an -ed ending. For example, *I was frightened by the movie*.

1 Experiences

Lead-in

- Books closed. Tell Ss that you want to tell them about an experience that happened a long time ago. Then tell them briefly (but dramatically!) the experience. For example, a trip you took with your family, learning to swim or ride a bike. Include how you felt.

- Tell Ss that even after many years, you remember the experience well.

- Tell Ss that in this unit, they will have the chance to share information about some of their memorable experiences.

A

- Tell Ss to look at the pictures on page 44. Ask a few focusing questions about the pictures. For example: *What's happening ? Where are the people? What are they doing? How do you think they feel?*
- Alternatively, write the questions on the board, and have Ss talk about the pictures in pairs. Then ask for a few volunteers to share their ideas with the class.
- Read the instructions and the comments aloud.
- Walk around the classroom, helping Ss as necessary while they do the activity.
- Elicit answers from Ss.

1A Answers *(left to right, top to bottom)*

Picture 1: C	Picture 4: D
Picture 2: F	Picture 5: B
Picture 3: E	Picture 6: A

B

- Read the instructions aloud.
- Read the words in the box aloud and have Ss repeat them.
- Point out the example in the chart. If necessary, explain the usage note on page 39 of this book.
- Remind Ss to add their own words.
- Walk around the classroom, helping Ss as necessary while they do the activity.
- Ask for a few volunteers to complete the sentences *It was . . . / I was . . .*

1B Answers

Describing experiences (*It was . . .*)	Describing feelings (*I was . . .*)
embarrassing	amazed
exhausting	excited
frightening	frustrated
interesting	interested
surprising	shocked
	terrified

C

- Have Ss form pairs.
- Read the instructions aloud.
- Point out the model language.
- Allow pairs time to share their experiences.
- Ask for a few volunteers to share their experiences with the class.

2 An experience when . . .

A

- Tell Ss they will now have a chance to talk about some of their important experiences.
- Read the instructions aloud.

- Have Ss read the types of experiences in the left column of the chart aloud. Explain or give examples of the experiences as appropriate.
- Walk around the classroom, helping Ss as necessary while they complete the chart.

B

- Have Ss form pairs. Read the instructions aloud.
- Call on two Ss to read the model conversation aloud. Explain that Ss should have a similar conversation using their information from the chart in Exercise A.
- Remind Ss that they should take notes on their partners' answers because they will need the information when they do Exercise C.
- Walk around the classroom, helping Ss as necessary while they do the speaking activity.

C

- Combine pairs to form groups of four or six.
- Read the instructions aloud.
- Point out the model language.
- Walk around the classroom, helping groups as necessary while they share information.
- Ask for a few volunteers to tell the class about a classmate's experience.

Focusing on language

Pages 46–47

1 Setting the scene

Usage note

make a new friend: Native speakers usually say *make a friend*, not *get a friend*.

A ◀)) ▶ 23

- Tell Ss that in this lesson they are going to hear about some people's memorable experiences
- Read the instructions aloud.
- Ask Ss to look at the pictures and try to imagine where the people are and what the experiences are.
- Have Ss share their guesses in pairs.
- Play the video or audio once or twice as needed. Encourage Ss to listen for keywords that will help them choose the correct pictures.
- Have Ss compare answers in pairs. Then elicit answers from Ss.

Tip

For lower-level classes, ask: *What do you see in the picture?* Elicit a few keywords for each picture.

1A Answers *(left to right, top to bottom)*

Picture 1: Ben
Picture 2: Grace
Picture 3: Sophie
Picture 4: extra picture

B 🔊 ▶ 23

- Tell Ss now to watch or listen for more details.
- Read the instructions aloud and allow time for Ss to read the information in the chart.
- Play the video or audio once or twice as needed.
- Have Ss compare answers in pairs. Then check answers with the class.

1B Answers

	Grace	Ben	Sophie
When	five, (a few years ago)	when he was (15)/13	(Junior high school), high school
Where	(a restaurant), concert	a stadium, (a golf course)	(Spain), Mexico
Feeling	It was so <u>amazing</u>.	He was <u>nervous</u> but thrilled.	She was <u>worried</u> about leaving.

C

- Tell Ss that now it's their turn to share some memorable experiences with their classmates.
- Have Ss form pairs. Read the instructions aloud.
- Call on individual Ss to read the experiences in the brown box aloud.
- Read the language in the *Setting the scene* box aloud and have Ss repeat it. Encourage them to use this language in their conversations.
- Call on two Ss to read the model conversation aloud.
- Walk around the classroom, helping Ss as necessary while they share their experiences.

Tip

For lower-level classes, give Ss a few minutes to think about their experiences and have them write notes before they begin.

2 Telling the story

Usage note

view: The noun *view* has both a literal and an abstract meaning. Its literal meaning refers to what can be seen from a specific location, e.g., *There's a nice view of the park from my window.* The more abstract meaning of view refers to an attitude or opinion about ideas or people, e.g., *My view of rock stars changed.*

A 🔊 ▶ 24

- Read the instructions aloud.
- Ask for volunteers to read the four sentences for each item aloud. Explain any unfamiliar language.
- Point out the example answer.
- Play the video or audio once or twice as needed.
- Have Ss compare answers in pairs.
- Check Ss' answers by asking for volunteers to say the sentences in the correct order.

2A Answers

Grace
_1_ Jack Thomas sat next to us.
_5_ My view of rock stars changed.
_3_ He asked about our interests.
_4_ He gave us concert tickets.
_2_ He ordered his food.

Ben
_4_ I washed the golf balls.
_2_ Mr. Olsen explained my duties.
_5_ I felt exhausted but happy.
_3_ I collected the balls with a cart.
_1_ Mr. Olsen encouraged me.

Sophie
_3_ I began to understand more.
_4_ I was able to talk with my host family.
_1_ I was confused.
_5_ I wanted to stay longer.
_2_ It was frustrating.

B 🔊 ▶ 24

- Read the instructions aloud.
- Read the time expressions aloud and have Ss repeat them.
- Play the video or audio once or twice as needed.
- Have Ss compare answers in pairs. Then check answers with the class.

2B   Answers

	Beginning
Ben	first of all
Grace	at first
Sophie	in the beginning

	Middle
Sophie	little by little
Grace	after a couple of minutes
Ben	soon after that

	End
Ben	when I finished
Sophie	in the end
Grace	finally

C

- Have Ss form pairs.
- Read the instructions aloud.
- Model the task by reading the model language aloud and asking for volunteers to complete Grace's story. Then tell pairs to do the same for Ben's and Sophie's stories. Remind Ss to use the time expressions.
- Walk around the classroom, helping Ss as necessary while they do the activity.
- Ask for volunteers to tell the stories to the class.
- Play ◀» ▶ 24 one more time, so that Ss can hear the original stories again.

Tip

For higher-level classes, have Ss close their books and tell the stories.

3   My experience

A

- Tell Ss to think about a memorable experience they have had. Ask them to think about when and where they had the experience and what exactly happened.
- Read the instructions and the example in the chart aloud.
- Remind Ss to write notes rather than complete sentences in the chart.
- Walk around the classroom, helping Ss as necessary.

B

- Read the instructions aloud and have Ss form small groups.
- Read the model language aloud and use the example notes in the chart to add information and complete the story.
- Allow time for Ss to look over their notes and silently practice telling the story.

- Walk around the classroom, helping groups as necessary as they share their experiences.
- Ask for a few volunteers to share their experiences with the class.

Organizing ideas

Pages 48–49

1   Patrick's memorable experience

Vocabulary

adventure: an unusual, exciting, and perhaps dangerous activity, trip, or experience

BCD: buoyancy control device, used for scuba diving

tropical: involving the warmest part of the earth

uneasy: feeling uncomfortable or worried

A

- Tell Ss to open their books to page 48 but have them cover Exercise B and page 49. Tell them to look only at the picture while you read the instructions and questions aloud.
- Elicit several responses to the questions.
- Tell Ss they are going to find out more information about Patrick's memorable experience in this lesson.

1A   Possible answers

It was a diving/snorkeling/boat trip.

He was amazed/excited/scared.

B

- Have Ss uncover their books and read the instructions aloud.
- Point out the brainstorming map on page 48 and the outline on page 49. Explain that Patrick decided not to use a few of his brainstorm topics in his final presentation outline.
- Walk around the classroom, helping Ss as necessary while they complete the activity.
- Ask for volunteers to say the topics they checked.

1B   Answers

When and where I had the experience
What happened at the beginning
What happened in the middle
What happened at the end

2 Patrick's presentation outline

A

- Read the instructions aloud. Explain that after Patrick made his brainstorming map he thought of a few more details he wanted to include in his presentation.
- Explain any unfamiliar language.
- Walk around the classroom, helping Ss as necessary while they complete the activity.
- If Ss have been working individually, have them compare their answers in pairs.

B ◄)) ► 25

- Read the instructions aloud. Make sure Ss understand that they will see or hear Patrick's whole presentation with the introduction and conclusion, but the outline is only for the body section.
- Play the video or audio and have Ss check their answers while they follow the outline.
- Check answers by reading through the outline aloud and eliciting the missing information.

2B Answers

A **When and where I had the experience**: said no at first, then agreed to try

B **What happened at the beginning**: had trouble but Mi Young encouraged me; heart pounding, scared, wanted to quit

C **What happened in the middle**: was near a coral reef with lots of fish; began to notice beautiful underwater world

D **What happened at the end**: passed my final test; he said, "I'm very proud of you."

C

- Read the instructions aloud and have Ss form pairs.
- Tell Ss that you will ask some of them to tell the class what they found out about their partner.

- Walk around the classroom, helping Ss as necessary while they complete the activity.
- Ask for a few volunteers to share what they found out about their partner.

Adding impact

Pages 50–51

1 Opener: mystery list

Lead-in

- Remind Ss that in Units 1–3, they learned three different ways to open and close a presentation. In this unit, they are going to learn another way they can do so.
- Read the explanation aloud.
- Have Ss look at the introduction outline at the top of the page.

A

- Read the instructions aloud.
- If necessary, have Ss look back at pages 48–49 to jog their memories.
- Have Ss share their ideas in pairs. Then elicit answers from Ss.
- Write Ss' ideas on the board.

B ◄)) ► 26

- Read the instructions aloud.
- Play the audio or video and have Ss complete Patrick's opener.
- Have Ss check their answers with their partner.
- Elicit the answers from Ss and write them on the board.

1B Answers

my dad . . . a turtle, a test . . . memorable experiences

2 Topic statement and preview

A

- Read the instructions aloud.
- Have Ss write in their answers.
- Have Ss compare their answers with one or two classmates.

B 🔊 ▶ 27

- Read the instructions aloud.
- Play the video or audio and have Ss check their answers.
- Elicit answers from Ss.
- If necessary, write the correct answers on the board for Ss' reference.

2B Answers

tell you about . . . describe . . . explain

Practice

A

- Read the instructions aloud.
- Have Ss look back at pages 46–47.
- Tell Ss that Grace, Ben, and Sophie added a mystery list opener to their presentations. The Ss' job is to complete their mystery lists.
- Have Ss add two or three items to each mystery list in the box.
- Walk around the classroom, helping Ss as necessary while they complete the activity.

Tip

If Ss have trouble thinking of items to add to the mystery lists in the box, brainstorm more items with the whole class. Alternatively, have Ss brainstorm more items in groups.

B

- Have Ss form pairs. Read the instructions aloud.
- Point out the useful language box and go over the language items with Ss.
- Give Ss a few minutes to choose one of the lists in the box and practice silently. Then ask Ss to present their opener to their partner.
- Walk around the classroom, helping Ss as necessary while they complete the activity.
- If Ss need more practice, have them change partners and repeat.

C

- Read the instructions aloud.
- Have Ss write their experience and mystery list in the box.
- Walk around the classroom, helping Ss as necessary while they complete the activity.
- Remind Ss to introduce their mystery list using the language in the box
- Have Ss present their opening mystery lists in pairs.
- Ask for a few volunteers to share their mystery list with the class.

3 Concluding signal and review

A 🔊 ▶ 28

- Read the instructions aloud. Have Ss look at the conclusion outline.
- Get Ss individually or in pairs to try to remember or guess the correct signal phrase.
- Play the video or audio and have Ss check their answers.
- Elicit answers from Ss and write them on the board.

3A Answer

So, in closing, I can say that

B 🔊 ▶ 29

- Read the instructions aloud.
- Have Ss individually or in pairs try to remember or guess the features from Patrick's review.
- Play the video or audio and have Ss write in their answers.
- Elicit answers from Ss.

3B Answers

helped me gain . . . taught me . . . gave me

4 Closer: "pass the mike"

- Read the explanation aloud. Remind Ss that *mike* means *microphone*. Mime the idea of passing the mike while explaining that it means giving someone else the opportunity to speak.

A

- Read the instructions aloud.
- Have Ss individually or in pairs try to remember or guess the missing words.
- Elicit answers from Ss and write them on the board.

B 🔊 ▶ 30

- Read the instructions aloud.
- Play the video or audio and have Ss check their answers.
- Elicit answers from Ss.

4B Answers

hearing about . . . encourages

A

- Have Ss form pairs. Read the instructions aloud.
- Read aloud the model language in the box. Have Ss repeat.
- Have Ss look back at Practice Exercises A and B on page 50.
- Walk around the room and help Ss as necessary while they are practicing their conclusion.

B

- Read the instructions aloud. Have Ss look at their notes for Practice Exercise C on page 50.
- Tell Ss to imagine that they have told their partner about their memorable experience from page 50, and now they want to end their presentation by passing the mike.
- Review the language in the box as necessary.
- Allow time for Ss to practice silently. Then ask them to present their closer to their partner.
- Walk around the classroom, helping Ss as necessary while they complete the activity.
- If Ss need more practice, have them change partners and repeat.

Developing presentation techniques

Pages 52–53

Vocabulary

bug: informal, non-scientific word for insect

filler: small word or phrase like *um, uh, well, you know* that speakers often add when they are not sure what to say next. They fill the silence, but it sounds casual

lorry: British English for truck

project your voice: speak loudly enough so people can hear you at a distance

tongue twister: a sentence or set of words that is difficult to say

volume: loudness

1 Using your voice

A

- Read the explanation at the top of the page aloud.
- Have Ss share their ideas about the pictures in pairs.
- Walk around the room, helping Ss as necessary.
- Elicit ideas from Ss and write them on the board.

1A   Possible answers *(pictures clockwise from top left)*

Problems

Picture 1: not speaking clearly, running words together

Picture 2: using lots of fillers so it sounds unprepared and boring

Picture 3: speaking too softly / not loud enough

Advice

Picture 1: speak more slowly and say words more clearly

Picture 2: prepare and practice more; don't use fillers

Picture 3: speak louder / project your voice

B 🔊 ▶ 31

- Read the instructions aloud.
- Make sure Ss understand that they need to listen for the features in the box when they watch or listen to Sophie.
- Play the video or audio and have Ss mark their answers.
- Have Ss compare their answers in pairs.
- Elicit answers from Ss.

1B   Answers

	Volume	Clear speech	Fillers
Version 1	😞	🙂	🙂
Version 2	🙂	😞	🙂
Version 3	🙂	🙂	😞

- Tell Ss that they can now have fun practicing using their voice effectively.
- Read the instructions aloud.
- Have Ss read each tongue twister silently.
- Practice each tongue twister with the whole class, saying them slowly and clearly, breaking them down into natural phrases as necessary.
- Have Ss form pairs around the room so there is some space between each pair.
- Make sure Ss in each pair are standing or sitting far enough apart so they have to project their voice to be heard.
- Walk around the room, helping Ss as necessary while they are practicing.
- If Ss need more practice, have them change partners and repeat.

2 Using stress to emphasize intensifiers

Lead-in

- Books closed. Tell Ss you are going to tell them
  about a memorable experience. Explain that you will
  tell the story twice and that they should listen to the
  difference between the two stories.
- Tell the story once without adding any of the
  intensifiers. Then tell the story again, adding the
  intensifiers *really*, *so*, *very*, *absolutely*, etc. and using
  slightly exaggerated stress and emphasis.
- When you finish, ask Ss which version of the story
  was more interesting to listen to and gave them
  a better understanding of your feelings about the
  experience. Elicit the intensifiers and write them
  on the board. Explain that these words are called
  intensifiers because they intensify or emphasize
  description and action words (adjectives and verbs)
  and that this makes the story more dramatic and
  interesting.

◀)) ▶ 32

- Read the instructions aloud.
- Play the video or audio once or twice as necessary.
- Have Ss compare answers in pairs.
- Elicit answers from Ss, and if necessary play the
  video or audio again to confirm.
- Walk around the room, helping Ss as necessary
  while they practice the sentences.

2 Answers

I was also <u>really thrilled</u> to earn my own money
We <u>couldn't believe</u> it. It was <u>so amazing</u>.
When I finished at 5 o'clock, I was <u>totally exhausted</u>,
but <u>happy</u>.
After that, I <u>completely forgot my fear</u>.
It was also <u>very scary</u> to be <u>so</u> far from home.
It was <u>absolutely terrifying</u>.

Practice

A

- Read the instructions aloud.
- Allow Ss time to read the note card, or read it aloud
  to the class.
- Walk around the room, helping Ss as necessary
  while they mark their answers.

- Have Ss compare their answers in pairs.
- Elicit answers from Ss and write them on the board.

B

- Have Ss work in the same pairs as in Exercise B.
- Read the instructions aloud.
- Point out the voice power tips. Read the tips aloud.
- Point out the model language at the bottom of the
  page.
- Walk around the room, helping Ss as necessary
  while they practice in pairs.
- Ask for a few volunteers to describe the scary
  experience to the class.
- When Ss finish, tell them that they are now ready
  to begin planning their own presentations about a
  memorable experience.

Present yourself!

Pages 54–55

1 Brainstorm

- Read the assignment and instructions aloud.
- As a reminder, have Ss look again at Patrick's
  brainstorming map on page 48.
- Give Ss enough time to partially or fully complete
  their brainstorming maps. Encourage Ss to include
  information and details they think their classmates
  will find interesting.
- Walk around the classroom, helping Ss as necessary
  while they complete the activity.

2 Organize

- Read the instructions aloud.
- Have Ss look again at Patrick's outline on page 49,
  as necessary.
- Point out that the Ss can add their own topics
  wherever they think they fit best into their outline.
- Give Ss time to think of a presentation title and
  complete the outline.
- Walk around the classroom, helping Ss as
  necessary.

3 Add impact

- Tell Ss that the above outline is for the body
  of their presentation. It's time to think about
  the introduction and conclusion to make the
  presentation complete and balanced.

- Read the instructions aloud.
- Elicit or remind Ss what type of opener and closer Patrick used in his presentation. (**Answers**: mystery list; pass the mike.) If necessary, have Ss look back at pages 50–51 and the model presentation on page 98.
- Give Ss enough time to complete their notes for the introduction and conclusion or ask Ss to complete them at home.

> **Tip**
>
> To reinforce Ss' learning about introductions and conclusions:
>
> ☐ Have Ss look at Patrick's model presentation on page 98. Ask them to underline the key language Patrick uses for his opener, topic statement, preview, conclusion signal phrase, review, and closer.
>
> ☐ Remind Ss of the type of openers and closers that Sophie, Ben, and Grace used in their model presentations in Units 1–3. Tell Ss that if they don't want to use the opener and closer from this unit, they can use ones from Units 1–3.

4 Make note cards

> **Tip**
>
> ☐ Depending on your available class time and student level, you may want to have Ss start this activity in class and finish it as homework.
>
> ☐ If Ss need more help making effective note cards, collect their cards and give written feedback on them to the Ss.

- Read the instructions aloud and have Ss look back at the tips on page 16.
- Have Ss make their final notes on note cards or, if that is not possible, on paper that is folded or cut to postcard size. Tell Ss that they should have three note cards: one for the introduction, one for the body, and one for the conclusion.
- Point out the note card tip on page 55 and read it aloud. If possible, use a note card yourself to show the Ss how this technique can be useful when speaking.
- If Ss will be using PowerPoint for their presentations, point out the PowerPoint tip on page 55 and read it aloud.

5 Practice and present

- Read the instructions aloud.
- Remind Ss that the more they practice their presentation, the more confident they will feel when they are speaking.
- Explain the format and time limit for Ss' presentations. Make sure Ss understand that they will be expected to use the language and presentation techniques they learned in Unit 2.

> **Tip**
>
> ☐ If time allows, have Ss form pairs or groups and take turns practicing their presentations in class. Suggest that Ss ask a classmate to time the length of their presentations, and encourage them to make suggestions to help improve their classmates' presentations.
>
> ☐ Depending on class size, you will need to determine the best format (group or whole class) and time limit for Ss' presentations. The student presentations in the course are intended to be 3–5 minutes, but you can of course change the timing to suit your situation.

- If you plan to have Ss use the **Outline worksheet** and **Peer evaluation form** (pages 80 and 83), or if you plan to use the **Assessment form** (page 84) during Ss' presentations, be sure to make the appropriate number of copies before Ss begin their presentations.
- When Ss finish their presentations, have them complete the **Self-evaluation** on page 104 in the Student's Book.

Unit 4 Expansion activities

Pages 86–87

Guide: Emma

Activity	Unit 4 page no.
1 Openers and closers	50–51
2 Voice power	53
3 Note card tips	55
4 PowerPoint tips	55
5 Unit goals checklist	44

1 Openers and closers

▶ 33, 34, 35 Ss watch Grace, Ben, and Sophie from the **Focusing on language** lesson. Each speaker has added an introduction and a conclusion to their topic. Ss watch and identify the type of opener and closer each speaker uses. Ss then watch Emma and check their answers.

1 Answers

Speaker	Openers	Closers
Grace	quotation	suggestion
Ben	question	statement about the topic's importance
Sophie	general statement	thought about the future

2 Voice power

▶ 36, 37 Ss review the voice power tips from page 53, then watch a section of Grace's and Ben's presentation from the **Focusing on language** lesson. Ss make notes as they watch, noticing what problems Grace and Ben have using their voices. Ss also write advice for the speakers to use their voices more effectively based on the tips on page 53. Ss then watch Emma and check their answers.

2 Answers

Speaker	Problems	Advice
Grace	spoke too softly, used lots of fillers	project voice; practice more and so avoid fillers
Ben	spoke too fast, didn't pause enough	speak more slowly and clearly; pause between sentences and phrases

3 Note card tips

▶ 38, 39, 40 In Exercise A, Ss read Grace's note card from her presentation in the **Focusing on language** lesson. They then watch a re-recorded version of Grace and notice what problems she has (because of her ineffective note card). In Exercise B, Ss rewrite Grace's note card using the tips on page 55, and compare their note card with Grace's note card on page 93. Ss then watch the original version of Grace presenting to notice how following the note card tips has helped her delivery. In Exercise C, Ss watch Emma and check their answers.

3 Answers

Version 1
Grace has to look at her note card a lot and she pauses frequently as she tries to find the right words in the note card. This is because her note card is written single-spaced, in full sentences, and without highlighting, bold, or caps to help her find keywords quickly.

Version 2
Grace delivers a good presentation. Her note card (see page 93) is written double-spaced, has keywords not full sentences, and uses color and caps. So she is able to find the information quickly.

4 PowerPoint tips

▶ 41, 42 This activity focuses on the PowerPoint tips from page 55. In Exercise A, Ss watch two versions of Patrick's introduction to his presentation about his memorable diving experience. Ss make notes as they watch the two versions, noticing what Patrick does badly and well when showing his slides. The first version is a re-recorded version, in which he doesn't show slides effectively because he doesn't follow some of the tips. The second version is the original version: Patrick makes effective use of PowerPoint. In Exercise B, Ss watch Emma and check their answers.

4 Answers

Version 1
Patrick uses only one slide, and on the slide he has all five pictures from the beginning. This makes it difficult for the audience to focus.

Version 2
Patrick shows six slides: one slide for each of the five pictures and finally one slide showing all five pictures. Each picture appears as he mentions it, so he is able to focus the audience's attention clearly. This follows the tip, "Less is more."

6 Unit goals checklist

Ss refer back to the unit goals on page 44 and complete a checklist to assess how well they have achieved the unit goals.

5 I'll show you how

Overview

All of the activities in the six lessons of this unit guide Ss to the main goal of planning and giving a 3–5 minute presentation about how to do or make something.

Lesson	Activities
Exploring the topic	Talking about types of skills and talents as well as why they are useful Interviewing classmates about their skills and talents
Focusing on language	Introducing the materials needed for a demonstration Giving clear instructions how to do or make something
Organizing ideas	Seeing how to brainstorm ideas and create an outline for a demonstration Watching or listening to Emma's demonstration about how to make a reusable storage container
Adding impact	Opener: asking problem-raising questions Closer: call to action
Developing presentation techniques	Using gestures for actions Checking understanding
Present yourself!	Brainstorming and organizing ideas for a demonstration about how to do or make something Giving a demonstration about how to do or make something

Exploring the topic

Pages 56–57

1 Skills and talents

Vocabulary

decorate: make a place (e.g., your home) more attractive with nice furniture, carpets, paintings, etc.

earn money: receive money as payment for work or services

entertain: keep people interested or amused

fitness: good physical health

impress: cause people to feel admiration or respect for you

juggle: throw several objects (balls, etc.) into the air, catch them, and keep them moving

knit: use two long needles and wool to make clothing

skills and talents: special abilities people have to do certain activities well. Skills are often acquired through learning or practice. Talents are often considered natural or something someone is born with

Usage note

do/practice vs. **play**: The verbs *do* and *practice* (not *play*) are used with most Eastern activities, such as yoga and martial arts. For example: do/practice yoga / tai chi / judo / karate

Lead-in

Books closed. Elicit the meaning of *skills and talents* by giving a few examples of your own skills and talents. Tell Ss that in this unit, they will share some of their own skills and talents with their classmates.

A

- Tell Ss to open their books to page 56. Read the instructions aloud.

- Read the categories and the example skills and talents in the chart aloud. Explain any unfamiliar language.
- Walk around the classroom, helping Ss as necessary, while they complete the chart.
- Write the categories from the chart on the board (Academic study, Cooking, Arts and crafts, etc.). Then ask for a few volunteers to come to the board and write their ideas under the appropriate categories.
- Take an informal survey by reading through the list of skills and talents on the board and asking Ss to raise their hands if they can do them.

1A Possible answers

Academic study: write essays, solve math problems, do science research

Arts and crafts: paint, do flower arranging, make jewelry

Clothing and fashion: sew clothes, design clothes, create fashion magazine

Computers and technology: edit videos, create a website, repair electronics

Cooking: cook French food, bake cookies, make pizza

Music and dance: play an instrument, sing, write music, dance salsa

Performing: dance, act, do stand-up comedy

Sports and fitness: run a marathon, play tennis, lift weights

---

B

- Read the instructions aloud.
- Read the reasons in the box aloud and explain any unfamiliar vocabulary.
- Call on two Ss to read the model exchange at the bottom of the page aloud.
- Have Ss share their ideas in pairs.
- Ask for a few volunteers to share their answers with the class.

2 Talent search

Vocabulary

greeting card: a card given for special occasions, such as birthdays

sew: make or repair clothes using thread and needles

A

- Tell Ss they will now find out about their classmates' skills and talents.
- Read the instructions aloud.
- Point out the model language and example in the chart.
- Have Ss read the skills in the left column of the chart. Explain any unfamiliar language.
- Make sure Ss understand that they should move around the classroom, asking a different S each question. If a classmate answers yes, they should write the classmate's name in the chart and then ask *Why do you think it's useful?* If a classmate answers no, they should ask a different person. Tell them they should write a classmate's name only once.
- Tell Ss they can use the reasons in the box in Exercise B on page 56 and their own ideas to complete the *Reason it's useful* column.
- Have Ss stand and move around to interview their classmates and complete the chart.

Tip

If class time is limited, finish this activity when you notice that most Ss have four or five skills or talents in the chart completed.

B

- Read the instructions aloud.
- Allow time for Ss to read the information they wrote in Exercise A.
- Point out the model language.
- Ask for a few volunteers to share their classmates' skills and talents with the class.

3 My talents

A

- Read the instructions aloud.
- Point out the written example in the chart.
- Give Ss time to complete the chart individually.
- Walk around the classroom, helping Ss as necessary.

B

- Have Ss form small groups.
- Read the instructions aloud.
- Point out the model language.
- Walk around the classroom, helping Ss as necessary as they complete the activity.
- Ask for a few volunteers to tell the class about one of their skills or talents.

1 Here's what you need

Vocabulary

avocado: a pear-shaped fruit with thick green or black skin, a large, round seed, and soft green or yellow flesh

demonstration: a presentation during which a person explains how to do something

fancy cooking: preparing a meal that is difficult and requires a lot of skill

glue stick: a solid, sticky substance in a plastic tube, used for joining things together

hard-boiled egg: an egg that is boiled long enough for the inside to become completely solid

loose: not tight, not fitting closely to the body

ripe: ready to be eaten

rubber band: a thin ring of rubber used to hold things together

wrap a gift: cover a gift in attractive paper

Lead-in

Books closed. Ask Ss to think about a skill that someone else has taught them how to do. Ask a few focusing questions about the experience of learning the skill. For example: *Who taught you the skill? Was it difficult to learn? How did you learn to do it? By listening to the person explain? By watching the person? What made the skill easy or difficult to learn? What helped you become successful?* Alternatively, write the questions on the board and have Ss discuss them in pairs. The goal of the activity is for Ss to understand the difference between explaining and demonstrating.

A ▶ 33

- Tell Ss to open their books to page 58. Explain that in this lesson, they are going to watch or listen to people demonstrating how to do or make something.
- Read the instructions aloud.
- Have Ss form pairs. Tell Ss to look at the pictures and guess what each demonstration's topic is and which comment goes with which picture.
- Allow time for Ss to mark their answers.
- Elicit guesses from Ss.
- Tell Ss to listen for keywords that will help them choose the correct demonstrations.
- Play the video or audio once or twice as needed.
- Have Ss compare answers in pairs. Then check the answers with the class.

1A Answers *(pictures left to right)*

Picture 1: 4	Picture 3: 2
Picture 2: 1	Picture 4: 3

B ◀)) ▶ 34

- Read the instructions aloud.
- Have Ss read the list of ingredients and materials. Explain any unfamiliar vocabulary.
- Make sure Ss understand that each speaker will say four things they need.
- Play the video or audio once or twice as needed.
- Have Ss compare answers in pairs. Then check the answers with the class.

1B Answers

P	avocados	B	milk carton
G	chair	P	onion
B	chopstick	G	pillow
S	colorful paper	S	Post-it slips
S	glue stick	P	ripe tomato
B	hard-boiled egg	G	rolled-up towel
P	lemon juice	S	round dish
G	loose clothing	B	rubber bands

C

- Read the instructions aloud.
- Have Ss read the demonstrations in the box and add their own idea.
- Explain to Ss that their classmates will try to guess their demonstration topic, so they should not show their information to anybody.
- Walk around the classroom, helping Ss as necessary while they choose their two demonstration topics and write the things that are needed.

D

- Tell Ss that they are now going to play a guessing game with the demonstrations they chose in Exercise C.
- Have Ss form groups of three or four.
- Read the instructions and the language in the box aloud. Encourage Ss to use this language in their groups.
- Ask for two volunteers to read the model conversation aloud.
- Walk around the classroom, helping Ss as necessary while they play the game.
- Ask for a few volunteers to play the guessing game with the whole class.

2 Follow the steps

Vocabulary

carton: a container made from cardboard or plastic, which often has milk or fruit juice

melted: turned liquid from heat or cooking

peel: remove the outer shell or skin of something

press: push something firmly

rectangle: a shape with four 90° angles and four sides, with opposite sides of equal length

slice: cut something into thin, flat pieces

A 🔊 ▶ 35

- Tell Ss that after deciding about the materials they need for their demonstrations, it's now time to think about the step-by-step instructions.
- Read the instructions aloud along with the captions under the pictures. Explain any unfamiliar language.
- Have Ss number the pictures individually then compare answers in pairs. You could also have Ss share their predicted order to establish a class consensus.
- Play the video or audio and have Ss check their guesses.
- Confirm answers by calling on individual Ss to say the steps in order.

2A Answers *(pictures left to right, top to bottom)*	
Picture 1: 4	Picture 5: 3
Picture 2: 8	Picture 6: 1
Picture 3: 5	Picture 7: 2
Picture 4: 7	Picture 8: 6

B 🔊 ▶ 35

- Tell Ss that they will watch or listen again, but this time for some key points.
- Read the instructions aloud.
- Have Ss read the notes on the note card.
- Play the video or audio and have Ss correct the mistakes.
- Have Ss compare answers in pairs. Then check the answers with the class.

C

- Tell Ss that they will now have the chance to practice giving instructions.
- Read the instructions aloud.
- Call on a student to read the example aloud.
- Walk around the classroom, helping Ss as necessary while they think of a drink or snack and write the instructions.

> ### Tip
> If Ss have trouble thinking of a drink or snack, have the whole class brainstorm some ideas and write them on the board.

> ### Grammar point
> When giving instructions or directions, we normally use imperative clauses or sentences. The usual word order is *verb + x*. We do not usually use the subject in an imperative clause, and the verb is in its base form. If necessary, go over the imperative form of verbs with Ss at this point in the lesson.

D

- Have Ss form pairs.
- Read the instructions aloud.
- Read the language in the box aloud, and have Ss repeat it. Tell Ss that this language helps make the order of the steps in the instructions clear for the listener. Encourage Ss to use it in their instructions.
- Point out the model language at the bottom of the page.
- Walk around the classroom, helping Ss as necessary while they give their instructions.
- Ask for a few volunteers to give their instructions to the class.

Organizing ideas

Pages 60–61

1 Emma's demonstration

> ### Vocabulary
> **cupboard**: a piece of furniture with a door, used to store things, usually on shelves
>
> **reusable**: can be used again
>
> **(un)screw**: tighten (untighten) something by twisting it
>
> **storage container**: something used to hold things that you want to keep
>
> **twist**: turn something repeatedly
>
> **uneven**: not level or smooth

A

- Tell Ss to open their books to page 60 but cover Exercise B and page 61. Tell them to look only at the picture while you read the instructions and questions aloud.
- Elicit several responses to the questions.
- Tell Ss they are going to find out more information about Emma's demonstration in this lesson.

B

- Have Ss uncover their books and read the instructions aloud.
- Point out the brainstorming map on page 60 and the outline on page 61. Explain that Emma decided not to use a few of her brainstorming topics in her final presentation outline.
- Walk around the classroom, helping Ss as necessary while they complete the activity.
- Ask for volunteers to say the topics they checked.

1B   Answers

Materials you need
Instructions
Key points to emphasize

2   Emma's presentation outline

Tip

Have Ss do this exercise in pairs, so they can help each other and share ideas.

A

- Read the instructions aloud. Explain that after Emma made her brainstorming map, she thought of a few more details she wanted to include in her presentation.
- Explain any unfamiliar language.
- Walk around the classroom, helping Ss as necessary while they complete the activity.
- If Ss have been working individually, have them compare their answers in pairs.

B 🔊 ▶ 36

- Read the instructions aloud. Make sure Ss understand that they will see or hear Emma's whole presentation with the introduction and conclusion, but the outline is only for the body section.
- Play the video or audio and have Ss check their answers while they follow the outline.
- Check answers by reading through the outline aloud and eliciting the missing information.

2B   Answers

A   Materials you need: kitchen towel
B   Instructions
    1   will need to use it in a few minutes
    2   be sure to cut in straight line around bottle
    4   important to push 5-6 cm of the bag through the section of the bottle
    5   fold food bag down over top of the section of the bottle
    6   remember to screw top on so it's tight

Tip

If Ss have trouble understanding Emma's presentation while watching or listening from only the outline, have them look at the full presentation on page 99 while they watch or listen again. Alternatively, if using the video, turn on the subtitles.

C

- Read the instructions aloud and have the Ss form pairs.
- Tell Ss that you will ask some of them to tell the class what they found out about their partner, so they should take notes of their partner's answers.
- Walk around the classroom, helping Ss as necessary while they complete the activity.
- Ask for a few volunteers to share what they found out about their partner.

Adding impact

Pages 62-63

Note

In Units 2-6, each unit focuses on one type of opener and closer to begin and end a presentation. In these units, it is the type of opener and closer that the speaker uses in their model presentation from the **Organizing ideas** lesson.

1   Opener: problem-raising questions

Lead-in

- Remind Ss that in Units 1-4, they learned four different ways to open and close a presentation. In this unit, they are going to learn another way they can use to do so.
- Read the explanation aloud.
- Have Ss look at the introduction outline at the top of the page.

A 🔊 ▶ 37

- Read the instructions aloud.
- If necessary, have Ss look back at pages 60-61 to jog their memories.
- Have Ss share their ideas in pairs. Then elicit answers from Ss.
- Play the video or audio and have Ss complete Emma's opener.
- Have Ss check their answers with their partner.
- Elicit answers from Ss and write them on the board.

are you concerned about . . . Do you buy . . .
expensive and troublesome

B

- Read the instructions aloud.
- Walk around the classroom, helping Ss as necessary while they write their questions.
- Have Ss share their questions in pairs.
- Ask for a few volunteers to share their questions with the whole class.

1B Possible answers

Do you often buy plastic water bottles?
Do you often throw away water bottles?
Do you throw away lots of plastic bags you don't need?
Would you like to save some money?
Would you like to learn a cool, cheap way to store things safely at home?

2 Topic statement and preview

A

- Read the instructions aloud.
- Have Ss write in their answers.
- Have Ss compare their answers with one or two classmates.

B ◀)) ▶ 38

- Read the instructions aloud.
- Play the video or audio and have Ss check their answers.
- Elicit answers from Ss.
- If necessary, play the video or audio of Emma's whole introduction again while Ss look at the model presentation on page 99.

2B Answers

I'm going to teach you . . . be able to . . . save . . . won't need to

Practice

A

- Read the instructions aloud.
- Walk around the classroom, helping Ss as necessary while they complete the activity.
- Ask for a few volunteers to share their questions.

Tip

If Ss have trouble thinking of opening questions for a demonstration about a scented candle, brainstorm some questions with the whole class. You can also get the brainstorming started by giving possible problem-raising questions yourself. For example:

Do you often feel stressed from your studies or work?

Do you need a way to reduce your stress?

Would you like to know how to make a simple but beautiful gift for a friend?

Would you like to be able to make an inexpensive but beautiful decoration for your room?

B

- Have Ss form pairs. Read the instructions aloud.
- Point out the useful language box and go over the expressions in the box with Ss. Encourage Ss to use them with their partner.
- Walk around the classroom, helping Ss as necessary while they complete the activity.
- Ask for a few volunteers to share their introductions.

3 Concluding signal and review

A ◀)) ▶ 39

- Read the instructions aloud. Have Ss look at the conclusion outline.
- Get Ss individually or in pairs to try to remember or guess the correct signal phrase.
- Play the video or audio and have Ss check their answers.
- Elicit answers from Ss and write them on the board.

3A Answer

So, that's how to

B ◀)) ▶ 40

- Read the instructions aloud.
- Get Ss individually or in pairs to try to remember or guess the features from Emma's review.
- Play the video or audio and have Ss write in their answers.
- Elicit answers from Ss.

3B Answers

saw . . . six . . . keep in mind

4 Closer: call to action

A

- Read the explanation and instructions aloud.
- Have Ss individually or in pairs try to remember or guess the missing words.
- Elicit answers from Ss and write them on the board.

B ◀))) ▶ 41

- Read the instructions aloud.
- Play the video or audio and have Ss write in their answers.
- Elicit answer from Ss.

4B Answer

encourage you to try it

Practice

A

- Have Ss form pairs. Read the instructions aloud.
- Read aloud the model language in the box. Have Ss repeat.
- Allow time for Ss to practice silently. Then ask Ss to give Emma's conclusion to their partner.
- Walk around the classroom, helping Ss as necessary.
- If Ss need more practice, have them change partners and repeat.

B

- Read the instructions aloud. Tell Ss that they will now make a conclusion for the demonstration about how to make a scented candle on page 62.
- Have Ss look back at Practice Exercises A and B on page 62.
- Allow time for Ss to practice silently. Then ask them to give their conclusion to their partner.
- Walk around the classroom, helping Ss as necessary.
- If Ss need more practice, have them change partners and repeat.

Developing presentation techniques

Pages 64-65

Vocabulary

case: a container used for protecting or storing things

chop: cut something into pieces

clockwise: moving around in the same direction as the pointers of a clock or watch

lid: a cover that can be lifted or removed from a container

pinch: tightly press something, usually between your finger and your thumb

spread: cover an object or area

stir: mix ingredients together, such as by moving a spoon in a circular movement

1 Gestures for actions

A

- Read the explanation at the top of the page aloud.
- Tell Ss that gestures can be important when giving a demonstration because they allow the audience to get the instructions using both their ears and their eyes. This helps the audience understand more clearly.
- Have Ss form pairs. Read the instructions aloud.
- Walk around the classroom, helping Ss as necessary while they share their ideas.
- Elicit ideas from Ss and write them on the board.

B

- Read the instructions aloud. Point out instructions A–F in the box. Explain any unfamiliar vocabulary.
- Have Ss stay in their pairs and do the matching activity. Walk around the classroom, helping as necessary.
- Elicit answers from Ss.
- Have Ss practice the gestures with their partner while saying the instructions.

Tip

Before Ss practice the gestures, demonstrate the gestures from the pictures while saying the instructions. Slightly exaggerate the gestures to make them very clear, and also get the Ss to do them with you.

1B Answers

Picture 1: F	Picture 4: A
Picture 2: B	Picture 5: E
Picture 3: C	Picture 6: D

A

- Read the instructions aloud.
- Read aloud instructions A–J and explain any unfamiliar vocabulary. If necessary, mime the gestures that naturally go with the instructions.
- Allow time for Ss to practice the gestures silently on their own.

B

- Have Ss form groups of three to four Ss. Read the instructions aloud.
- Walk around the classroom, helping Ss as necessary while they do the activity.
- Ask for a few volunteers to demonstrate the instructions with gestures to the class.

Tip

- ☐ To make this practice activity more realistic, ask Ss to stand up and use good presentation posture when it's their turn to speak.
- ☐ Remind Ss to make eye contact with their group members when they are speaking, using the read silently-look-up-speak technique (Student's Book page 17, Exercise 2B).

2 Checking understanding

A 🔊 ▶ 42

- Read the explanation at the top of the page. Clarify as necessary.
- Ask Ss if they remember how Emma checked that the audience was following her demonstration.
- Read the instructions aloud.
- Play the video or audio and have Ss write in their answer.
- Elicit the answer from Ss.

2A Answer

Is that part clear?

B 🔊 ▶ 43

- Read the instructions aloud.
- Play the video or audio and have Ss write in their answer.
- Elicit the answer from Ss.

2B Answer

Are there any questions?

Practice

Vocabulary

ribbon: a long narrow strip of material used to tie things together or as a decoration

triangle shape: having three sides

upside down: having the part that is usually at the top turned to be at the bottom

wrinkle: a small fold in cloth or a small line in the skin

A

- Have Ss form pairs. Read the instructions aloud.
- Point out the language for checking understanding at the bottom of page 65.
- Have Ss look back at their instructions for Exercise C on page 59.
- Walk around the classroom, helping Ss as necessary while they do the activity.

B

- Read the instructions aloud.
- Have Ss read the instructions in the box for how to wrap a gift. Explain any unfamiliar vocabulary.
- Allow time for Ss to check two instructions for checking understanding.
- Remind Ss that for the instructions with key points, they should use the expressions from the box on page 59 (*Make sure that you . . . ; It's important to . . .* etc.)
- Point out the demonstration tips at the bottom of page 65.
- Walk around the classroom, helping Ss as necessary while they do the activity in pairs.
- If Ss need more practice, have them change partners and repeat.
- Ask for a few volunteers to demonstrate checking understanding to the class.
- When Ss finish, tell them that they are now ready to begin planning their own demonstration of how to do or make something.

Present yourself!

Pages 66–67

1 Brainstorm

- Read the assignment and instructions aloud.
- As a reminder, have Ss look again at Emma's brainstorming map on page 60.
- Give Ss enough time to partially or fully complete their brainstorming maps. Encourage Ss to include information and details they think their classmates will find interesting.
- Walk around the classroom, helping Ss as necessary while they complete the activity.

2 Organize

- Read the instructions aloud.
- Have Ss look again at Emma's outline on page 61, as necessary.
- Point out that the key points are important points that are easy to forget or get wrong.
- Give Ss time to think of a presentation title and complete the outline.
- Walk around the classroom, helping Ss as necessary.

3 Add impact

- Tell Ss that the above outline is for the body of their presentation. It's time to think about the introduction and conclusion to make the presentation complete and balanced.
- Read the instructions aloud.
- Elicit or remind Ss what type of opener and closer Emma used in her presentation. (**Answers:** problem-raising questions; call to action.) If necessary, have Ss look back at pages 62 and 63 and the model presentation on page 99.
- Give Ss enough time to complete their notes for the introduction and conclusion or ask Ss to complete them at home.

4 Make note cards

- Read the instructions aloud and have Ss look back at the tips on page 16.
- Have Ss make their final notes on note cards or, if that is not possible, on paper that is folded or cut to postcard size. Tell Ss that they should have three note cards: one for the introduction, one for the body, and one for the conclusion.
- Point out the note card tip on page 67 and read it aloud. If possible, use a note card yourself to show Ss how this technique can be useful when giving a demonstration.
- If Ss will be using PowerPoint for their presentations, point out the PowerPoint tips on page 67 and read them aloud.

5 Practice and present

- Read the instructions aloud.
- Remind Ss that the more they practice their presentation, the more confident they will feel when they are speaking.
- Explain the format and time limit for Ss' presentations. Make sure Ss understand that they will be expected to use the language and presentation techniques they learned in this unit.

- If you plan to have Ss use the **Outline worksheet** and **Peer evaluation form** (pages 81 and 83), or if you plan to use the **Assessment form** (page 84) during Ss' presentations, be sure to make the appropriate number of copies before Ss begin their presentations.
- When Ss finish their presentations, have them complete the **Self-evaluation** on page 105 in the Student's Book.

Unit 5 Expansion activities

Pages 88–89

Guide: Jason

Activity	Unit 5 page no.
1 Openers and closers	62–63
2 Gestures for actions	64
3 Emphasizing key points	59 and 65
4 PowerPoint tips	67
5 Unit goals checklist	56

1 Openers and closers

▶ 43, 44, 45 Ss watch Grace, Ben, and Sophie from the **Focusing on language** lesson. Each speaker has added an introduction and a conclusion to their topic. Ss watch and identify the type of opener and closer each speaker uses. Then they watch Jason and check their answers.

1 Answers

Speaker	Openers	Closers
Grace	a surprising fact	a call to action
Ben	a problem-raising question	emphasizing the topic's specialness
Sophie	a proverb	a request for others to share: pass the mike

2 Gestures for actions

▶ 46, 47 Ss watch two versions of a section of Emma's demonstration about how to make a reusable storage container. Ss complete a checklist as they watch the two versions, noticing which steps Emma supports by making clear, effective gestures for actions. The first version is a re-recorded version in which she does not use gestures to reinforce her actions for the instructions. She also appears quite bored and speaks with a rather bored, monotonous intonation. The second version is the originally recorded version from the **Organizing ideas** lesson, in which she uses clear gestures. In Exercise B, Ss watch Jason and check their answers.

2 Answers

Version 1
Emma uses some gestures to show the steps but they are not clear or effective. This could be because she seems bored and not interested in demonstrating clearly to the audience.

Version 2
Emma uses clear, effective gestures to show each step.

> **Tip**
>
> Although the focus is on the use of gestures, you may want to elicit Ss' ideas about Emma's attitude and have Ss explain their reasons for their ideas (lazy gestures, "bored" intonation, etc.)

3 Emphasizing key points

▶ 48, 49 This activity focuses on the expressions for emphasizing key points (see page 59). Ss first watch a section of Ben's demonstration about how to make a heart-shaped egg and match the expressions he uses with the key points he wants to emphasize. Ss then watch Jason and check their answers.

3 Answers

Make sure that the short side is not wider than 8 centimeters.

Be careful not to press down too hard or the egg will break.

Be sure to keep the rubber bands in place at least 10 minutes.

4 PowerPoint tips

▶ 50, 51 This activity focuses on the PowerPoint tips from page 67. In Exercise A, Ss watch two versions of a section of Emma's demonstration. Ss complete a checklist as they watch the two versions, noticing how effectively she uses her slides. The first version is a re-recorded version, in which her slides are not designed well and she does not show them effectively. The second version is the originally recorded version: Emma makes effective use of PowerPoint. In Exercise B, Ss watch Jason and check their answers.

4 Answers

	Version 1	Version 2
1 Number of slides used	1	2
2 Key verb of each instruction highlighted?	No	Yes
3 Colors used for highlighting words?	No	Yes
4 Pauses given for audience to read slide?	No	Yes
5 More effective use of PowerPoint slides		✔

5 Unit goals checklist

Ss refer back to the unit goals on page 56 and complete a checklist to assess how well they have achieved those goals.

6 Screen magic

Overview

All of the activities in the six lessons of this unit guide Ss to the main goal of planning and giving a 3-5 minute presentation to review a movie or TV show they have seen.

Lesson	Activities
Exploring the topic	Quizzing classmates about their film and TV knowledge Talking with classmates about familiar movies and TV shows
Focusing on language	Talking about the features of movies and TV shows: genre, plot, setting, special effects, acting, cinematography, dialogue Watching or listening to four short reviews of a movie or TV show
Organizing ideas	Seeing how to brainstorm ideas and create an outline for a movie review Watching or listening to Jason's movie review of *Man of Steel*
Adding impact	Opener: interesting facts Closer: recommendation
Developing presentation techniques	Sentence stress Phrasing with pauses
Present yourself!	Brainstorming and organizing ideas for a movie review Giving a 3–5 minute presentation to review a movie or TV show

Exploring the topic

Pages 68–69

1 Film and TV quiz

Vocabulary

boarding school: a school with rooms where students stay instead of living at home

character: a person represented in a movie, play, or story

feature (n): noticeable or important characteristic of a movie (plot, setting, etc.)

feature (v): show someone or something as the most important or most obvious

play: perform as a character in a movie or play. For example, *She played the queen.*

setting: the time and place of a story

solve a crime: to figure out who did the action that is against the law

Usage note

North Americans usually use the words *movie* and *TV show*, whereas in Britain the words *film* and *TV programme* are more often used. In Australia and New Zealand, *movie* and *film* are both used interchangeably, and *TV show* is more common than *TV programme*. Documentaries are usually referred to as *film* in all countries.

Lead-in

- Books closed. Ask Ss some general questions about their movie and TV show preferences. For example: *Do you enjoy watching movies? How often do you watch a movie? Do you have any favorite TV shows? What are some recent popular movies and TV shows? Have you seen any of them?*

- Ask for a few volunteers to say whether they liked the movies and why or why not. Alternatively, show a few photos of well-known movie stars and ask Ss to think of movies they starred in.

- Tell Ss that in this unit, they will talk about different types of movies and TV shows as well as discuss what they like and dislike about them.

A

- Tell Ss to open their books to page 68. Read the instructions aloud.
- Ask Ss to read the quiz questions and answer choices on their own. Explain any unfamiliar language.
- Have Ss form pairs and ask each other the quiz questions. Tell them not to look at the back of the book for the answers until they have finished the quiz.
- Have Ss compare answers in pairs before they check their own answers on page 93.
- Finish by taking an informal class survey to find out who knew the most answers and which questions were easiest or most difficult.

B

- Have Ss stay in their pairs from Exercise A.
- Read the instructions aloud. Tell Ss they must also write at least three answer choices for each question. The answer choices should not be too easy or too difficult.
- Walk around the classroom, helping Ss as necessary while they write their questions.

Tip

☐ For lower-level classes, provide or elicit some other examples of movie-related quiz questions and write them on the board. For example: *How many Harry Potter movies are there?*

   a 6   b 7   c 8   (Answer c)

☐ Some Ss may think of good movie / TV show questions but not be sure of the correct answer. If appropriate, allow Ss to use their smartphones to do a web search for the answer.

- Point out the model language. Then have pairs join to form groups of four.
- Walk around the classroom, helping Ss as necessary while they ask their quiz questions.
- Ask for a few volunteers to ask their quiz questions to the class.

2 Screen highlights

Vocabulary

awesome: extremely good, exciting, or wonderful

battle: a fight between armed forces

chase: hurry after in order to catch someone or something

confusing: difficult to follow or understand

costume: clothing worn by actors in a movie or play

---

lead: main or most important character

special effects: images in a movie that appear real but are created by artists and technical experts

spectacular: very exciting or interesting because of being large or extreme

---

Culture tip

Movie titles
Movies often have very different titles when they are distributed internationally, so some Ss may not recognize the original titles. Check the local titles of movies and be ready to give some extra information to help Ss recognize the movies.

A

- Tell Ss they will now have a chance to talk about some movies they know.
- Read the instructions aloud.
- Have Ss read the features in the left column of the chart. Explain any unfamiliar language.
- Point out the example in the chart.
- Walk around the classroom, helping Ss as necessary while they complete the chart.

B

- Have Ss form pairs.
- Read the instructions aloud.
- Have two Ss read the model conversation aloud. Tell Ss to have a similar conversation using the information in the chart.
- Remind Ss that they should take notes on their partner's answers because they will need that information when they do Exercise C.
- Walk around the classroom, helping Ss as necessary while they do the speaking activity.

C

- Read the instructions aloud.
- Ask for a few volunteers to tell the class about one of their partners' movies.

Tip

If time allows, lead a brief discussion about the movies Ss have seen. Ask how many Ss have seen the movies, what the movies and TV shows from the chart are about, and what Ss liked and disliked about them.

---

3 My favorites

A

- Read the instructions aloud.
- Point out the example in the chart.
- Walk around the classroom, helping Ss as necessary while they complete the chart.

B

- Have Ss form pairs. Read the instructions aloud.
- Point out the model language.
- Have pairs share their information.
- Ask for a few volunteers to tell the class about one of their favorite movies or TV shows.

Focusing on language

Pages 70–71

1 What's it about?

Vocabulary

cinematography: the art and methods of using the cameras in making a movie

create: make something new or imaginative

criminal: a person who has done something against the law

documentary: a film based on factual information

monster: an imaginary frightening creature

noble: having a high social rank, especially from birth

plot: the plan or main story of a film, TV show, or book

ruled by: controlled by someone or something with more power than you

survive: continue to live after a dangerous event or situation

zombie: a dead person who is brought back to life without the ability to speak or move easily

Movie genres

The traditional genres or types of films / TV shows are: **action, adventure, comedy, documentary, drama, horror, musical, romance, science fiction (sci-fi), suspense/thriller**.
However, film reviews often combine more than one genre to form a more specific term, for example: **romantic comedy, magical adventure, sci-fi adventure, historical drama, police comedy, spy thriller**.

Lead-in

- Tell Ss the names of a few well-known movies and elicit the genre (comedy, horror, etc.) of each one. Have Ss work in pairs to think of all the movie types they know along with the name of a movie for each type. Call on a few Ss to share their answers with the class.
- Tell Ss that in this lesson, they are going to focus on different types of movies and their stories.

A 🔊 ▶ 44

- Tell Ss to open their books to page 70.
- Read the instructions aloud.
- Read the answer choices aloud. Explain any unfamiliar language.
- Allow time for Ss to mark their answer choices.
- Play the video or audio and have Ss check their answers.
- Confirm answers by asking for a few volunteers to say the correct information.

1A Answers

	Life of Pi	The Walking Dead	The Hunger Games	Game of Thrones
Type of movie or TV show	Magical adventure	Horror drama	Sci-fi adventure	Fantasy
Setting	India and a small boat	America	Panem in the future	Westeros
Plot	a tiger	has been taken over by zombies	compete in a fight-to-the-death game	fight for control of the Iron Throne

B 🔊 ▶ 44

- Read the instructions aloud. Have Ss take out a sheet of paper to write their answers.
- Tell Ss just to write brief notes, not complete sentences.
- Play the video or audio and have Ss write their answers.
- Have Ss compare their notes in pairs, then elicit answers from Ss.

1B Possible answers

Life of Pi
Pi's father owned zoo; Pi's family and animals were on boat, going to Canada; storm sinks boat; tiger kills other animals; Pi and tiger accept each other

The Walking Dead
Main character, Rick Grimes, a sheriff; woke up from coma; goes to Atlanta to search for wife and son; finds them; fights against zombies and survivors

The Hunger Games
Teenage boy and girl chosen every year; main character Katniss Everdeen, from District 12; volunteers instead of younger sister; goes with boy called Peeta to Capitol

Game of Thrones
Three connected storylines; one about seven noble families who are fighting for control of Iron Throne; one about freezing winter and monsters; one about former rulers of Westeros, who want to take back kingdom

C
- Read the instructions aloud.
- Point out the example on the note pad. Ask Ss if they know what musical it is. Elicit guesses from volunteers. (**Answer:** *Les Misérables*)
- Provide additional examples as necessary. For example: *It's about a boy with special powers who goes to a strange school to learn how to become a wizard.* (**Answer:** Harry Potter)
- Explain to Ss that their classmates will try to guess their movie or TV show, so they should not show their notes to anybody.
- Walk around the classroom, helping Ss as necessary while they write their notes.

D
- Have Ss form groups of four or five.
- Read the instructions aloud.
- Read the language in the box aloud, and if necessary have Ss repeat it. Encourage Ss to use this language in their group guessing game.
- Call on two Ss to read the model conversation aloud.
- Walk around the room helping Ss as necessary while they play the game.
- Ask for a few volunteers to give their clues to the class, and have the rest of the class try to guess the movie or TV show.

2 Screen reviews

Vocabulary

complicated: having many parts or characters, or the story is organized in a way that is difficult to follow

dialogue: conversation between the characters in a movie

disappointing: not as good as hoped or expected

fantastic: very good

powerful: having a strong effect

predictable: happening in a way that is expected so you can guess the ending

realistic: seeming real or possible

soundtrack: the music that is played during a movie

stunning: very beautiful

A
- Read the instructions aloud.
- Read the words to describe movie features in the box aloud, and if necessary have Ss repeat them. Explain any unfamiliar language.
- Have Ss add words of their own. Then have them compare ideas in pairs.
- Call on a few Ss to share their adjectives. Write them on the board and ask Ss to say the movie features that their adjectives go with.

2A Possible answers

acting: (un)believable, excellent, (un)natural, realistic, shocking, terrible

cinematography: beautiful, spectacular, stunning

dialogue: funny/hilarious, moving, powerful, realistic, ridiculous, thought-provoking

plot: boring, complicated, confusing, exciting, fast/slow-moving, funny/hilarious, original, predictable, ridiculous, scary/terrifying, thought-provoking

special effects: beautiful, (un)believable, disappointing, fantastic, spectacular, stunning

Tip

To help Ss practice the vocabulary, have them form pairs or groups and think of movies that fit each vocabulary item. Then have them share their ideas with the class.

B ◀)) ▶ 45
- Tell Ss that they will now watch or listen to reviews of the four movies / TV shows on page 70.
- Read the instructions aloud.
- Read the features in the chart aloud and elicit or explain the meaning of each one.
- Play the video or audio and have Ss circle their answers.
- Have Ss compare their answers in pairs. Then check the answers with the class.

C ◀)) ▶ 45
- Read the instructions aloud. Tell Ss that now they need to listen for more specific details.

- Play the video or audio and have Ss write their answers.
- Have Ss compare their answers in pairs. Then check the answers with the class.

1B and C   Answers

	Movie Features		
Emma	cinematography ☺	special effects ☺	plot ☹
	fantastic	spectacular, realistic	slow moving, confusing
Patrick	plot ☹	acting ☹	dialogue ☹
	ridiculous, unoriginal	terrible, unnatural	unrealistic, unbelievable
Grace	acting ☺	plot ☺	cinematography ☹
	excellent	fast moving, exciting	disappointing, irritation
Ben	plot ☺	acting ☺	cinematography ☺
	complicated, fascinating	fantastic	stunning

3 My movie review

- Have Ss form pairs. Read the instructions aloud.
- Point out the example answer in the box and the model language at the bottom of the page.
- Walk around the classroom, helping Ss as necessary while they do the speaking activity.
- Ask for a few volunteers to share their information with the class. Encourage other Ss to give their opinions if they have seen the movie and whether they agree about the features.

Organizing ideas

Pages 72–73

1 Jason's movie review

Vocabulary

adopt: take another person's child legally into your own family to raise as your own child

cast: all the actors in a movie or show

destroy: damage something in a violent way

direct: tell actors in a movie or play how to act their roles

infancy: the first stage of life as a very young child

flashback: a short part of a movie that describes past events

preview: an advance showing or details of a movie before its official opening

protect: keep someone or something safe from injury, damage, or loss

recommendation: advice or suggestion

struggle: work hard to do something that is difficult

Lead-in

- Books closed. Ask Ss how they usually decide in advance what movies or TV shows to watch. Find out if Ss ever read or watch movie reviews.
- Ask Ss what information is usually included in a full movie review. Write their ideas on the board.
- Tell Ss that in this lesson, they are going to see how to organize information for a full movie review.

A

- Tell Ss to open their books to page 72, but have them cover Exercise B and page 73. Tell them to look only at the pictures while you read the instructions and questions aloud.
- Elicit several responses to the questions.

B

- Have Ss uncover their books. Read the instructions aloud.
- Point out the brainstorming map on page 72 and the outline on page 73. Explain that Jason decided not to use a few of his brainstorm topics in his final presentation outline.
- Walk around the classroom, helping Ss as necessary while they complete the activity.
- Ask for a few volunteers to say the topics they checked.

1B   Answers

Setting
Plot
What I liked
What I didn't like

2 Jason's presentation outline

Tip

Have Ss do this exercise in pairs, so they can help each other and share ideas.

A

- Read the instructions aloud. Explain that after Jason made his brainstorming map, he thought of a few more details he wanted to include in his presentation.
- Explain any unfamiliar language.
- Walk around the classroom, helping Ss as necessary while they complete the activity.
- If Ss have been working individually, have them compare their answers in pairs.

B 🔊 ► 46

- Read the instructions aloud. Make sure Ss understand that they will see or hear Jason's whole presentation with the introduction and conclusion, but the outline is only for the body section.
- Play the video or audio and have Ss check their answers while they follow the outline.
- Check answers by reading through the outline aloud and eliciting the missing information.

Tip

If Ss have trouble following Jason's presentation while watching or listening from only the outline, have them look at the full presentation on page 100 while they watch or listen again. Alternatively, if using the video, turn on the subtitles.

C

- Read the instructions aloud and have Ss form pairs.
- Tell Ss that you will ask some of them to tell the class what they found out about their partner, so they should take notes of their partner's answers.
- Walk around the classroom, helping Ss as necessary while they complete the activity.
- Ask for a few volunteers to share what they found out about their partner.

Adding impact

Pages 74–75

Note

In Units 2-6, each unit focuses on one type of opener and closer to begin and end a presentation. In these units, it is the type of opener and closer that the speaker uses in their model presentation from the **Organizing ideas** lesson.

1 Opener: interesting facts

Lead-in

- Remind Ss that in Units 1–5, they learned different ways to open and close a presentation. In this unit, they are going to learn about another way they can do so.
- Read the explanation aloud.
- Have Ss look at the introduction outline at the top of the page.

A

- Read the instructions aloud.
- If necessary, have Ss look back at pages 72–73 to jog their memories.
- Elicit answers from Ss about Jason's questions about Superman.
- Have Ss write other possible quiz questions Jason could ask to begin his presentation .
- Have Ss share their ideas in pairs, then elicit answers from Ss.
- Write Ss' questions on the board and elicit any answers that Ss know.

B 🔊 ► 47

- Tell Ss they will now compare their opening questions with Jason's.
- Read the instructions aloud.
- Play the video or audio and have Ss complete Jason's opener.
- Have Ss check their answers with their partner.
- Elicit the answers from Ss and write them on the board.

2 Topic statement and preview

 ► 48

Vocabulary

agent: a person who works for the government as a spy or to fight crime.

buried: put in the ground and covered with earth

Pompeii: ancient city in Italy that was destroyed by a volcano 2,000 years ago

- Read the instructions aloud.
- Play the video or audio and have Ss write their answers.
- Have Ss compare their answers in pairs. Then check the answers with the class.
- If necessary, play the video or audio of Jason's whole introduction again while Ss look at the model presentation on page 100.

2B Answers

want to talk about . . . 2013 . . . an action . . . directed by . . . stars

Practice

A
- Read the instructions aloud.
- Allow time for Ss to read the information about the movie and TV show in the boxes. Explain any unfamiliar language.

B
- Have Ss form pairs. Read the instructions aloud.
- Point out the language items in the box, and if necessary read them aloud with the Ss.
- Have Ss in each pair choose one of the boxes (Pompeii or NCIS) to use for their opener.
- If Ss need more practice, have them change partners and repeat, this time using the information in the other box.
- Ask for a few volunteers to give their opener to the class.

3 Concluding signal and review

A ► 49
- Read the instructions aloud. Have Ss look at the conclusion outline box.
- Have Ss individually or in pairs try to remember or guess the correct signal phrase.

- Play the video or audio and have Ss check their answers.
- Elicit answers from Ss and write them on the board.

3A Answer

So, what's my final rating of *Man of Steel*?

B ► 50
- Read the instructions aloud.
- Have Ss individually or in pairs try to remember or guess Jason's rating of *Man of Steel*.
- Play the video or audio and have Ss write in their answers.
- Elicit answers from Ss.

3B Answers

four stars out of five . . . plot . . . special effects . . . action scenes . . . cast

4 Closer: recommendation

A
- Read the explanation and the instructions aloud.
- Have Ss individually or in pairs try to remember or guess Jason's recommendation.
- Elicit answers from Ss and write them on the board.

B ► 51
- Read the instructions aloud.
- Play the video or audio and have Ss check their answers.
- Elicit answers from Ss.

4B Answers

definitely worth . . . recommend . . . on a big screen

Practice

Vocabulary

rating: a score or evaluation of how good something is compared with other things of the same type

worth watching: enjoyable or useful, not a waste of time

A

- Have Ss form pairs. Read the instructions aloud.
- Read aloud the language items in the box. Explain any unfamiliar language.
- Allow time for Ss to practice silently. Then have them give Jason's conclusion to their partner. Remind Ss to include his signal phrase, his rating, and his recommendation.
- Walk around the classroom, helping Ss as necessary while they complete the activity.
- If Ss need more practice, have them change partners and repeat.

B

- Read the instructions aloud.
- Give Ss time to think of a movie or TV show and have them make some notes on a piece of paper.
- Allow time for Ss to practice silently. Then ask them to give their conclusion for their movie to their partner.
- Walk around the classroom, helping Ss as necessary while they complete the activity.
- If Ss need more practice, have them change partners and repeat.

Developing presentation techniques

Pages 76–77

1 Sentence stress

Vocabulary

astronaut: a person who is trained for traveling in a spacecraft

infect: cause a disease in someone by introducing a virus or bacteria

prisoner: a person who is under the control of someone else and not physically free

rescue: save someone from a dangerous or harmful situation

Lead-in

- Tell Ss that you are going to give a short summary of a movie plot and that you are going to say it twice. The Ss should tell you which version sounds more natural. For example: *A group of criminals from outer space tries to save the galaxy from a villain who wants complete power.* (*Guardians of the Galaxy*; released 2014)
- Say the sentence the first time with flat, even intonation, *not* stressing the content words. Then say the sentence again with the content words naturally stressed or with slight exaggeration to make the point.

- Try to elicit from Ss that the only difference between the two versions of the sentence was your stress and that the second version was much more natural and easy to follow because you used natural sentence stress in English.
- Write the sentence on the board and say it again stressing the content words (underlined here): *A group of <u>criminals</u> from <u>outer space</u> tries to <u>save</u> the <u>galaxy</u> from a <u>villain</u> who wants <u>complete power</u>.* Elicit from Ss which words were stressed.
- Tell Ss to open their books to page 76. Read the explanation aloud. Make sure Ss understand the difference between content words and function words.

A 🔊 ▶ 52

- Read the instructions aloud.
- Allow time for Ss to read the extracts and underline the stressed words.
- Play the video or audio and have Ss check their answers.
- Have Ss compare their answers in pairs
- Elicit answers from Ss.

1A and 2A   Answers

Emma
After <u>seven years</u> / as a <u>prisoner</u> in <u>Iraq</u>, / Brody is <u>rescued</u> / and <u>returns</u> to the United States as a <u>war hero</u>.

Patrick
It takes place in <u>Tokyo</u> / during the <u>rainy season</u>, / and it's the story of 15-year-old <u>Takao</u>, / who dreams of becoming a <u>shoemaker</u>.

Grace
<u>Brad Pitt</u> plays a <u>United Nations official</u>, / who travels <u>all over</u> the <u>world</u> trying to stop <u>zombies</u> / from <u>infecting everyone</u>.

Ben
It stars <u>Sandra Bullock</u> and <u>George Clooney</u> / as <u>astronauts</u> on the <u>space shuttle Explorer</u>, / which is <u>damaged</u> / while they're on a <u>mission</u> in outer space.

B

- Read the instructions aloud
- Have Ss underline the stressed words on their own.
- Have Ss compare their answers and read the extract aloud in pairs
- Walk around the room, helping Ss as necessary. Notice which Ss are reading the extract with natural English sentence stress.
- Ask for one of the Ss who used natural sentence stress to read the passage to the class.
- If necessary, read the passage aloud yourself.

Practice

A

- Read aloud the instructions and the headings in the box.
- Remind Ss that the setting is when and where the movie or show takes place, and the plot is the main idea of the story in a sentence or two.
- Walk around the classroom, helping Ss as necessary while they write their information and underline the words they think should be stressed.
- Allow time for Ss to practice on their own.

B

- Have Ss form pairs. Read the instructions aloud.
- Point out the model language at the bottom of the page.
- Walk around the classroom, helping Ss as necessary while they talk about their movie or TV show.
- If Ss need more practice, have them change partners and repeat.
- Ask for a few volunteers to tell the class about their movie or TV show.

2 Phrasing with pauses

Lead-in

- Read the explanation at the top of the page aloud, pausing where appropriate.
- Ask Ss if they noticed how many times and where you paused.
- Read the explanation again, with the same pauses and elicit from Ss where you paused. You also may want to also write it on the board. For example: *You can keep your audience's attention / by using brief pauses. / Use them to separate complete thoughts, / phrases within a sentence, / and at the end of a sentence.*

A ◀))) ▶ 52

- Read the instructions aloud. Tell Ss that they are going to watch or listen to the same four extracts from page 76, but this time they should notice where the speakers pause for natural phrasing.
- Play the video or audio and have Ss mark their answers.
- Have Ss compare their answers in pairs
- Elicit Ss' answers, and if necessary play the video or audio again to confirm.

2A Answers

see **1A and 2A Answers** *on page 66*

B

- Have Ss form pairs. Read the instructions aloud.
- Walk around the classroom, helping Ss as necessary while they complete the activity.

Practice

A

- Read the instructions aloud.
- Have Ss read the extract in the box and draw lines for the pauses.
- Allow time for Ss to practice on their own.
- Have Ss in pairs practice saying the extract naturally with pauses.

Tip

- ☐ For lower-level classes who may have trouble with phrasing with pauses, read the extract in the box yourself and have the Ss draw lines for the pauses as you read.
- ☐ Remind Ss to use the read silently-look up-speak technique when they are saying the extract aloud to their partner.

B

- Read the instructions aloud.
- Point out the sentence stress and phrasing tips. Read them aloud.
- Allow time for Ss to mark the pauses for their information in Practice A on page 76.
- Have Ss form pairs or small groups.
- Walk around the room, helping Ss as necessary while they complete the activity. Notice which Ss are speaking with natural pauses for phrasing.
- Ask for one or two of the Ss who used natural pauses to describe their movie or TV show to the class.
- When Ss finish, tell them that they are now ready to begin planning their own presentation for a movie or TV show review.

Present yourself!

Pages 78–79

1 Brainstorm

- Read the assignment and instructions aloud.
- As a reminder, have Ss look again at Jason's brainstorming map on page 72.
- Give Ss enough time to partially or fully complete their brainstorming maps. Encourage Ss to include information and details they think their classmates will find interesting.
- Walk around the classroom, helping Ss as necessary while they complete the activity.

2 Organize

- Read the instructions aloud.
- Have Ss look again at Jason's outline on page 73, as necessary.
- Tell Ss they can add their own topics wherever they think they fit best into their outline.
- Give Ss time to think of a presentation title and complete the outline.
- Walk around the classroom, helping Ss as necessary.

Tip

If Ss need more help organizing their outlines, collect their outlines and give written feedback on them to the Ss.

3 Add impact

- Tell Ss that the above outline is for the body of their presentation. It's time to think about the introduction and conclusion to make the presentation complete and balanced.
- Read the instructions aloud.
- Elicit or remind Ss what type of opener and closer Jason used in his presentation. (**Answers:** interesting facts; recommendation.) If necessary, have Ss look back at pages 74 and 75 and the model presentation on page 100.
- Give Ss enough time to complete their notes for the introduction and conclusion or ask Ss to complete them at home.

Tip

To reinforce Ss' learning about introductions and conclusions:

☐ Have Ss look at Jason's model presentation on page 100. Ask them to underline the key language Jason uses for his opener, topic statement, preview, conclusion signal phrase, review, and closer.

☐ Remind Ss of the type of openers and closers that Sophie, Ben, Grace, Emma, and Patrick used in their model presentations in Units 1–5. Tell Ss that if they don't want to use the opener and closer from this unit, they can use the ones from Units 1–5.

4 Make note cards

Tip

☐ Depending on your available class time and student level, you may want to have Ss start this activity in class and finish it as homework.

☐ If Ss need more help making effective note cards, collect their cards and give written feedback on them.

- Read the instructions aloud and have Ss look back at the tips on page 16.
- Have Ss make their final notes on note cards or, if that is not possible, on paper that is folded or cut to postcard size. Tell Ss that they should have three note cards: one for the introduction, one for the body, and one for the conclusion.
- Point out the note card tips on page 79 and read them aloud. If possible, use a note card yourself to show Ss how the first tip can be useful when speaking.
- If Ss will be using PowerPoint for their presentations, point out the PowerPoint tips on page 79 and read them aloud.

5 Practice and present

- Read the instructions aloud.
- Remind Ss that the more they practice their presentation, the more confident they will feel when they are speaking.
- Explain the format and time limit for Ss' presentations. Make sure Ss understand that they will be expected to use the language and presentation techniques they learned in Unit 2.

Tip

☐ If time allows, you may want to have Ss form pairs or groups and take turns practicing their presentations in class. Suggest that Ss ask a classmate to time the length of their presentations, and encourage them to make suggestions to help improve their classmates' presentations.

☐ Depending on class size, you will need to determine the best format (group or whole class) and time limit for Ss' presentations. The student presentations in the course are intended to be 3–5 minutes, but you can of course change the timing to suit your situation.

- If you plan to have Ss use the **Outline worksheet** and **Peer evaluation form** (pages 82 and 83), or if you plan to use the **Assessment form** (page 84) during Ss' presentations, be sure to make the appropriate number of copies before Ss begin their presentations.
- When Ss finish their presentations, have them complete the **Self-evaluation** on page 106 in the Student's Book.

Unit 6 Expansion activities

Pages 90–91

Guide: Sophie

Activity	Unit 6 page no.
1 Openers and closers	74–75
2 Sentence stress	76
3 Phrasing with pauses	77
4 Note card tips	79
5 PowerPoint tips	79
6 Unit goals checklist	68
Final thoughts about *Present Yourself*	

1 Openers and closers

▶ 52, 53, 54 Ss watch Emma, Patrick, Grace, and Ben from the **Focusing on language** lesson. Each speaker has added an introduction and a conclusion to their topic. Ss watch and identify the type of opener each speaker uses. They then watch the speakers' conclusions and complete a chart for the closer (rating and recommendation) that each speaker gives. Finally, Ss watch Sophie and check their answers.

1A Answers

Speaker	Opener
Emma	a mystery list
Grace	a general statement
Ben	a quotation

1B Answers

Speaker	Rating	For its ...
Emma	3 stars out of 5	amazing special effects
Grace	2 thumbs up	fast-moving plot, great acting
Ben	8 out of 10	fascinating plot, stunning scenery

Recommendation

Emma	in a movie theater or on a big HD screen in a dark room.
Grace	rent it and see it at home with your friends.
Ben	watch every episode and download any that you miss.

2 Sentence stress

▶ 55 Ss review Exercise 1B on page 76 and then record themselves saying the same extract, based on the stressed words they underlined. Ss then watch Jason saying the same extract and compare his version with theirs.

2B Answers

As a <u>child</u>, Clark discovers that he has <u>special powers</u>, and later he tries to find out where he <u>comes</u> from. In his travels, he meets the reporter <u>Lois Lane</u> and he <u>communicates</u> by <u>hologram</u> with his father, <u>Jor-El</u>. Clark <u>learns</u> that he was sent to <u>Earth</u> to bring <u>hope</u> to <u>mankind</u>.

3 Phrasing with pauses

▶ 56 Ss review Practice A on page 77 and then record themselves saying the same extract, based on the phrasing lines they drew. Ss then watch Jason saying the same extract and compare his version with theirs.

3B Answers

Man of Steel is set on the planet Krypton / and on Earth, / including the United States and Canada. / The movie covers Superman's life / from infancy to his 30s. / The movie tells the story of Superman's origins – / how he becomes / Superman. / At the beginning, / Krypton is dying, / so its leader, Jor-El, / sends his baby son, Kal-El, / to Earth. / Kal-El is adopted by kindly farmers in Kansas / and they name him Clark.

4 Note card tips

▶ 57, 58 In Exercise A, Ss watch two versions of Patrick's presentation from the **Focusing on language** lesson. The first version is a re-recorded version of Patrick, in which he does not follow the note card tips from page 79. The second version is the original version of Patrick presenting, in which he uses his note card effectively because he follows the tips on page 79. Ss fill in a checklist while they watch both versions. In Exercise B, Ss watch Sophie and check their answers.

4 Answers

	Version 1	Version 2
1	About 10 times	Once or twice
2	No	Yes
3	No	Yes
4	No	Yes

Patrick is clearly unprepared and so not confident in Version 1. He forgets what to say, has to look at his cards a lot, and the cards are in the wrong order. In Version 2, Patrick has to look at his cards only once or twice. He is confident because he has clearly practiced a lot.

5 PowerPoint tips

▶ 59, 60 This activity focuses on the PowerPoint tip from page 79. In Exercise A, Ss watch two versions of a section of Jason's presentation from the **Focusing on language** lesson. Ss complete a checklist as they watch the two versions, noticing how effectively Jason uses his slides. The first version is a re-recorded version, in which his slides are not designed very well and he does not show them effectively. The second version is the original version: Jason makes effective use of PowerPoint. In Exercise B, Ss watch Sophie and check their answers.

5   Answers

	Version 1	Version 2
Number of fonts used	7	2
Number of colors used	7	2
More effective use of PowerPoint slides		✔

In Version 1, too many colors and fonts make Jason's slide hard to read and confusing. In Version 2, two colors and two easy-to-read fonts make Jason's slide clear and effective.

6 Unit goals checklist

Ss refer back to the unit goals on page 68 and complete a checklist to assess how well they have achieved those goals.

Final thoughts about *Present Yourself*

As this is the final unit in *Present Yourself*, Ss are invited to reflect on their experience and preferences while using the course. The four questions give Ss an opportunity to refresh their memories about the topics and presentations they have covered, without the need for you to highlight them in the classroom. These questions could also form the basis for an end-of-semester or end-of-year in-class rounding-up session, with Ss in pairs or small groups sharing their ideas, preferences, and opinions about the course. Alternatively, you could ask Ss to write their answers to the four questions and submit them to you. Either way, orally or in writing, the Ss' responses could offer you some useful feedback, which will help your course planning for next semester.

Unit 1 Language summary

Personal profiles

age	interests
dislikes	likes
fashion style	music
hang-out spot	occupation
hometown	personality type

Personal information questions

Are friends an important part of your life?
What kind of people do you get along with the best?
What do you usually do with your friends?
Who has been your friend the longest?
Who is your newest friend?
In what ways are you and your friends similar or different?
Do you have a best friend?
How would you complete the sentence below?
A good friend is someone who . . .

Words to describe people

a morning person	laidback and relaxed
a night person	messy
a workaholic	moody
active	neat and tidy
adventurous	outgoing
funny	quiet and serious

Interests and activities

chatting online	playing sports
going out to eat	seeing a movie
going shopping	singing karaoke

Talking about interests and activities

He loves / hates / can't stand playing the guitar.
He likes / doesn't like watching sports.
She enjoys / doesn't enjoy going to museums.
She's into / isn't into hard rock.
We both love / like / enjoy action movies.

Introduction parts

Greeting
Opener
Topic statement
Preview

Conclusion parts

Signal phrase
Review
Closer
Thanks

Opener: introducing a quotation or proverb

I'd like to begin with a quote (from) . . .
There's a saying/proverb (in . . .) about . . .
A wise person once said: . . .

Closer: thought or comment about the future

Well, after listening to me, now you know about . . .

Unit 2 Language summary

Words to describe places

big and spacious	noisy
crowded	quiet and peaceful
historical	small and cozy
lively	traditional
messy	trendy
modern	unusual

Words to describe size and shape

huge	short
large	square
little	thick
narrow	thin
oval	tiny
round	wavy

Types of places

amusement park	fitness club
beach	movie theater
bookstore	museum
café	public garden
dance club	shopping mall

Activities

check email or Facebook
relax and think
enjoy some fresh air
get away from it all
watch people
listen to music
do homework
take pictures
play computer games

Describing places

It's	big and spacious / busy on weekends.
It has	a new computer / great views.
There's	a ticket machine / a comfortable sofa.
There are	lots of windows / tall trees.

Talking about how often you go there

I go there at least once a week / once or twice a month / a few times a year.

Talking about activities

I go there a lot to hang out with friends.
It's a great place to shop for clothes.
When I'm there, I go bowling.
I (really) like/enjoy/love window-shopping there.
I (really) spend a lot of time there.

Opener: introducing a general statement

I think everyone has/does/likes/wants . . .
I believe most people have/do/like /want . . .
I'm sure that all students / most of us / many of you / we all . . .

Conclusion

Signal

All in all, . . .	To sum up, . . .
To recap, . . .	To summarize, . . .

Closer: making a closing invitation

I really hope you get the chance to visit . . . sometime.
I'd like to invite you to come to . . . in the (near) future.
If you have the chance to go to . . . one day, please do.
I'm positive/confident/certain/sure you'll have a great time / love it / find it special / enjoy it there / too / as well.

Unit 3 Language summary

Possessions

a book collection	a pair of jeans
a coin	a scented candle
a guitar	a souvenir
a handicraft	a trophy

Reasons possessions are important

brings back memories
brings good luck
helps you relax
is old or handmade
makes life more fun or interesting
represents an achievement

Words to describe possessions

attractive	faded	smooth
beautiful	floral	soft
big	flowers	special
checked	gold	stiff
checks	leather	striped
colorful	lovely	stripes
comfortable	natural	swirls
cool	old	thick
cotton	perfect	thin
dark	rough	useful
dots	round	wide
dotted	simple	wood
earthy	small	

Describing possessions

It's beautiful/attractive/cool/lovely/colorful.
It's small/round/soft/faded.
It has flowers/checks/strips/dots on it.

It's floral/checked/striped/dotted.
It's made of leather/cotton/gold/wood.

Explaining a possession's history and use

It was a birthday gift / graduation present.
I got it from my dad / as a gift / in Seoul / when I started/finished/visited . . .
I've had it for eight / a few years.
I've had it since 2005 / high school / I was 12.
I use it to drink my coffee every day / record my thoughts.
I use it when I hang out in my room.

Show-and-tell expressions

As you can see, it's striped here on the front.
Can you (all) see that it's faded here on the top?
If you look here, you'll notice that it has a hole / **there's a** patch here on the back.
I'm not sure (if) you can see it clearly, so I've shown it here on this slide.

Opener: introducing an opening question

I'd like to begin with a (simple) question.
I want to start by asking you a (simple) question.
I'm going to start by asking you a (simple) question.
To begin, here's a question for you (to think about).

Conclusion

Signal

All in all, . . .	To sum up, . . .
In conclusion, . . .	To summarize, . . .
To recap, . . .	

Closer: emphasize why something is special

It's not (only/just) because . . .
Rather / Instead / Most of all / Above all, it's because . . .

Unit 4 Language summary

Words to describe experiences and feelings

amazed/amazing
embarrassed/embarrassing
excited/exciting
exhausted/exhausting
frightened/frightening
frustrated/frustrating
interested/interesting
shocked/shocking
surprised/surprising
terrified/terrifying

Memorable experiences

An experience . . .
   that changed my attitude
   that gave me confidence
   that made me laugh a lot
   when I achieved something difficult
   when I did something for the first time
   when I did something scary
   when I learned something new
   when I made a new friend
   when I made an important decision
   when I saw something amazing
   when I won an award

Time expressions

first of all / at first / in the beginning
little by little / after a couple of minutes / soon after that
when I finished / in the end / finally

Setting the scene

   It happened in 2010.
   This happened to me when I was in high school.
   I had this experience a few years ago / during my second year of college.
   One day, I was in Europe and I lost my passport.
   We were at a mall when the lights went out.
   We were sightseeing when I was robbed.

Opener: mystery list

   What do these things have in common?
   What is the connection between them?
   How do these items go/fit together?
   How are these things connected?
   They are all part of one of the most memorable/meaningful experiences I've had in my life /
   ever had.

Conclusion

   Signal

   Let me end by saying . . .
   So, in closing, I can say that . . .
   To conclude, . . .
   To sum up, ...

   Closer: pass the mike

   Now, I hope listening to my memorable experience encourages you to share yours.
   Well, I hope hearing about my prized possession inspires you to present yours.
   Now, I hope presenting/sharing my favorite place motivates you to tell us about yours.

Unit 5 Language summary

Skills and talents

bake a cake
create a blog
do yoga
draw a cartoon character
juggle
knit a scarf
make an origami animal
make your own greeting cards
memorize new vocabulary
play the piano

Reasons skills and talents are useful

You can . . .

decorate your home	entertain people
earn or save money	make gifts for people

It can . . .

help you relax	improve your health
impress people	make work or study easier

Tasks

make a cup of tea	make an omelet
make a milkshake	wrap a gift

Presenting the materials you need

Before you begin, you need . . .
Here's what you need to start: . . .
For this, you should have . . .

Giving instructions

OK, let's get started.
Right, here's how to do it.
First / Next / Then / Now / After that / Finally . . .
Make sure that (you) . . .
It's important to / Be sure to / Don't forget to . . .
There are only two/three/four more steps to go.

Checking understanding

Are there any questions?
Does anyone want me to repeat that step?
Is that part clear?
Would you like to see that again?

Opener: asking problem-raising questions

Tell me, do you . . . ?
I'd like to know: have you ever . . . ?
Please raise your hand: are you . . . ?

Conclusion

Signal

So, now you can . . .
So, now you have a simple way to . . .
So, now you know how to . . .
So, that's how to . . .

Review

As you saw / I showed you / I demonstrated, . . .

Closer

I hope you'll try it yourself when . . .
I encourage you to try it for yourself the next time you . . .

Unit 6 Language summary

Types of movies / TV shows

action
documentary
fantasy
historical drama
horror drama
love story
magical adventure
musical
police comedy
romantic comedy
sci-fi adventure
suspense thriller

Adjectives to describe movie / TV show features

beautiful	original
(un)believable	powerful
complicated	predictable
confusing	(un)realistic
disappointing	shocking
fantastic	spectacular
fast/slow moving	stunning
(un)natural	

Movie / TV show features

acting	setting
cinematography	special effects
dialogue	soundtrack
plot	

Talking about movies / TV shows

It's a romantic comedy / love story.
It's an action film/movie.
The story takes place in France in . . .
It's set in an airplane . . .

It's about a prisoner who agrees to . . .
It follows a CIA agent who believes . . .
Brad Pitt **plays** a UN worker who tries to . . .
It's based on a true story.

Opener: interesting facts quiz

Did you know that . . . ?
It may surprise you that . . .
Here's an interesting/surprising fact: . . .

Introducing a movie or TV show

Man of Steel **was released/made in** 2013.
It was directed by Zack Snyder.
It stars Henry Cavill as Superman.

Conclusion

Signal

So, what do I think of *Man of Steel*?
So, is *Man of Steel* **worth watching?**
So, what's my final rating of *Man of Steel*?

Rating

Overall, I give it three stars out of five / two thumbs up / eight out of ten.

Recommendation

It's definitely/really (not) worth seeing.
I recommend that you see it on a big screen / rent it.
My recommendation is don't waste your time.
I think this is a movie/show you really should/shouldn't see/miss.

Unit 1 Outline worksheet

Presenter: _____

A good friend

Introduction

Opener

_____

Name of the presenter's friend: _____

Body

A How they met

_____

_____

B Things in common

_____

_____

_____

C How they are different

_____

_____

_____

D What they do together

_____

_____

_____

E Other information

_____

_____

Conclusion

Closer

_____

Something else I'd like to know about the presenter's friend

_____

_____

_____

Unit 2 Outline worksheet

Presenter: _____

A favorite place

Introduction

Opener

_____

Name of the place: _____

Body

A General description

_____
_____

B What it has

_____
_____
_____

C Interesting features

_____
_____
_____

D When the presenter goes there

_____
_____
_____

E What the presenter does there

_____
_____

Conclusion

Closer

_____

Something else I'd like to know about the place

_____
_____
_____

Unit 3 Outline worksheet

Presenter: _____

A prized possession

Introduction

Opener

_____

The possession: _____

Body

A Description: size, shape, texture, pattern, shape, etc.

_____

_____

B Condition

_____

_____

_____

C History: how and when the presenter got it

_____

_____

_____

D How the presenter uses it

_____

_____

_____

E Other information

_____

_____

Conclusion

Closer

_____

Something else I'd like to know about the possession

_____

_____

_____

Unit 4 Outline worksheet

Presenter: _____

A memorable experience

Introduction

Opener

_____

The experience: _____

Body

A When and where the experience took place

_____
_____

B What happened at the beginning of the experience

_____
_____
_____

C What happened in the middle of the experience

_____
_____
_____

D What happened at the end of the experience

_____
_____
_____

E Other information

_____
_____

Conclusion

Closer

_____

Something else I'd like to know about the experience

_____
_____
_____

Unit 5 Outline worksheet

Presenter: _____

A demonstration

Introduction

Opener

_____

How to: _____

Body

A Materials needed

_____

_____

B Instructions and key points

1 _____

_____

2 _____

_____

3 _____

_____

4 _____

_____

5 _____

_____

6 _____

_____

C Other information

_____

_____

Conclusion

Closer

_____

Something else I'd like to know about the demonstration topic

_____

_____

_____

Unit 6 Outline worksheet

Presenter: _____

A movie / TV show review

Introduction

Opener

_____

The movie / TV show: _____

Body

A Setting

_____

_____

B Plot

_____

_____

_____

C What the presenter liked

_____

_____

_____

D What the presenter didn't like

_____

_____

_____

E Other information

_____

_____

Conclusion

Final rating: _____

Recommendation: _____

Something else I'd like to know about the movie / TV show

_____

_____

_____

Peer evaluation form

Read each statement. Circle ☺, 😐, or ☹. Then write comments that will help you improve next time.

Presenter: _____

Unit / Topic: _____

The presenter greeted the audience and smiled at the beginning.	☺ 😐 ☹
The presenter chose an interesting, suitable topic for the audience.	☺ 😐 ☹
The presentation's introduction had an opener, topic statement, and preview.	☺ 😐 ☹
The body of the presentation included enough interesting details about the topic.	☺ 😐 ☹
The presenter used the vocabulary and language from this unit effectively.	☺ 😐 ☹
The presentation's conclusion had a signal phrase, review, and closer.	☺ 😐 ☹
The presenter spoke clearly and was easy to understand.	☺ 😐 ☹
The presenter maintained good posture and made eye contact.	☺ 😐 ☹
The presenter thanked the audience at the end.	☺ 😐 ☹

One thing that the presenter did well: _____

_____

_____

One suggestion that I have for the presenter: _____

_____

_____

Assessment form

Presenter: _____

Unit / Topic: _____

Feature	Score
The presenter greeted the audience appropriately at the beginning.	1 2 3 4 5
The presentation's introduction had an opener, topic statement, and preview.	1 2 3 4 5
The body of the presentation included enough interesting details about the topic and was supported by appropriate visual aids or PowerPoint slides, as required.	1 2 3 4 5
The presenter used the vocabulary and language from this unit effectively.	1 2 3 4 5
The presentation's conclusion had a signal phrase, review, and closer.	1 2 3 4 5
The presenter spoke loudly enough, clearly, and with appropriate intonation.	1 2 3 4 5
The presenter used note cards and made eye contact.	1 2 3 4 5
The presenter maintained good posture and used appropriate gestures.	1 2 3 4 5
The presenter thanked the audience at the end.	1 2 3 4 5
The presentation was within the required length.	1 2 3 4 5

TOTAL: _____ / 50

What the presenter did well	
Suggestions for improvement	

Getting Ready

🔊 ▶ 1

Emma: Hello everyone. Welcome to *Present Yourself!* I'm Emma. In this course, we'll show you lots of ways to develop your speaking skills, so that you can give effective presentations with confidence. Today, I'm going to tell you about six steps you can take to plan and prepare your presentations. First, think about your audience and choose a presentation topic that fits their needs and interests. Second, brainstorm lots of ideas and information about your topic and put them into a brainstorming map. Third, organize your supporting topics and details into an outline with an introduction, a body, and a conclusion. The fourth step is to think of a good way to begin and end your presentation to add impact. You need a good opener at the beginning to "hook" the audience's attention, and you need a strong closing last sentence to end your presentation. We'll show you ways to do this during the course. That brings us to step number five: make note cards to help you remember what you want to say when you give your presentation. Finally, the last step is the most important. You should practice your presentation lots of times with your note cards and a clock or watch to time your presentation. These six steps will help to make your presentation planning much easier. Good luck in this class and in this course!

🔊 ▶ 2

Maricel: Good morning. I'm Maricel Lopez. My first name is Maricel, but actually my friends and family call me Mar. That's my nickname and I like it, so please call me Mar. I'd like to tell you a little bit about my hometown and family.

I'm from Cebu in the Philippines. It's a large island in the south of the country. Cebu has some beautiful beaches and also delicious mangos. I love mangos! We also have a very colorful festival every year in January. My family is quite big: we have seven people – my mom and dad, my four brothers and sisters, and me. We live in a small house near the sea. My father is a fisherman, and he works very hard. I have two younger brothers and two younger sisters. I'm the oldest. My youngest brother is Bobby, and he is six.

Now you know a little bit about my hometown and family. I'm so excited to be in this class, but also a little nervous. I really want to get more confident in English. I also want to make new friends in this class. Thank you.

🔊 ▶ 3

Patrick: Hello, I'm Patrick. I'm sure you all want to give great presentations, so today I'm going to tell you about five useful presentation techniques. They will really help you make a strong impact on your audience. OK, so what are the five techniques?

First is managing anxiety. Of course, before a presentation, it's normal to be nervous. So try to relax. Take three or four slow, deep breaths – like this. And smile. That really helps. Also, don't apologize to your audience. Never say, "Sorry, I'm very nervous." Try to appear confident. Next is good posture. How you stand is important. Place your feet 20 to 30 centimeters apart. That's about shoulder width. This really helps your balance. And don't sway from side to side – like this. That makes the audience uncomfortable. One more thing: don't lean on a table or desk; it looks too casual. Third is eye contact. That means looking at your audience when you speak. This really helps you to connect. Try to look at each person in the audience for a few seconds, and then look at someone else. Remember also to look at all sections of the room – front, back, left, and right. Another useful presentation technique is using gestures. You can use your hands and arms to help you emphasize key points. But it's important to keep your arm movements clear, simple, and natural. You should also make sure your movements are not too quick or sudden. And don't use gestures too much. The last technique today is projecting your voice. That means speaking loudly and clearly so everyone can hear and understand you. Just imagine that you're speaking to the people at the back of the room. However, don't shout. That makes the audience very uncomfortable.

So, now you know five useful presentation techniques: reduce anxiety, maintain good posture, make eye contact, use gestures, and project your voice. With these techniques, you'll become a much better presenter. I promise!

Unit 1 A good friend

🔊 ▶ 4

Patrick: I've known Nick since junior high school, and he's one of my best friends. What kind of person is he? Well, I guess you can say he's pretty quiet and serious – exactly the opposite of me. He likes spending a lot of time at home with his music, and he's not really into parties or hanging out. He's also not very neat and tidy. In fact, his room is a real mess: the floor is covered with his clothes. It kind of looks like a typhoon hit his room!

Emma: My friend Hana is really fun. We only met a year ago at our part-time job, but already we feel like sisters. How would I describe her? Well, she enjoys going to parties, hanging out with friends, and meeting new people. Actually, we're both pretty outgoing and sociable, so that's good. She also likes trying new things and learning about new and different ideas. That definitely makes life more interesting!

Jason: I met Sami three years ago when we were first-year students in university in London. His personality type? Let's see, definitely not the lazy type, that's for sure. Sami's incredibly active and energetic – we both are – so that's probably why we became friends. He always wants to be outdoors, playing sports, hiking, running, whatever. He also likes to tell jokes, so my friends and I are always laughing when we hang out with him.

🔊 ▶ 5

Patrick: Nick's totally into classical music, and he loves playing the piano – usually two or three hours a day. I don't really enjoy classical music, but I'm a big fan of blues music. So when Nick and I meet up, around once a month, I usually take him to one of my favorite live blues clubs. Actually, I think he's starting to like blues. Occasionally, I go with him to a classical concert in the city, but I always fall asleep in the middle of it!

Emma: Hana and I both love singing karaoke and going out to eat, especially to restaurants we've never tried before. That's what we often do on Saturdays. We go out for dinner, then sing karaoke for a couple of hours. Hana likes Italian food, and I love Thai food, so we take turns choosing a different restaurant. That means it's always an adventure. And the karaoke is really fun, even though we're both terrible singers!

Jason: Sami loves trying new things – especially extreme sports. Right now he's into paragliding and kitesurfing. That's a bit too much for me. I prefer running, cycling, and swimming. They're a lot safer and really good exercise. Actually, Sami and I are training together for a triathlon race. That's what we do twice a week, on Wednesday evening and Sunday afternoon. After our training, we usually go to the nearest coffee shop to plan our next session.

🔊 ▶ 6

Sophie: Good morning everyone. I'm Sophie, and I'm happy to speak with you today. In Nigeria, there's a saying about friendship: Hold your friends in both hands. I really like this idea, and today I'd like to tell you about my best friend. I'll tell you how we met, what we have in common, how we're different, and what we do together. After you have listened to me, you'll know why I hold my friend in both hands.

Kate and I met four years ago in our high school dance circle, and we became friends almost immediately. I guess that's because we have a lot in common, for example, our family, our personality, and the things we like to do. Kate doesn't have any brothers or sisters, and I'm an only child too. Also, our mothers are both elementary school teachers. So, how would I describe Kate? Well, she's very easygoing and laid-back – just like me! We don't get upset very often, and we don't argue much. We're also both very positive, optimistic people. Our number one passion is hip-hop music and fashion. You can guess that when you see us because we both always dress in street-style clothes. As I said, Kate and I have a lot in common, but we're also different in some ways – like our studies, our reading habits, and some of

the things we like. Kate's very smart, and she's a top student – especially in math. But I'm the opposite: I'm terrible at math! I'm much better in English, and I love reading novels. But Kate hates reading books: she only reads music magazines. She's also a night person and hates getting up early. On weekends, she sleeps until noon. I'm more of a morning person. I always get up before 8 a.m. Kate and I see each other a lot on campus, of course, but we also get together on weekends. We usually hang out at the mall and have a coffee at Starbucks. We also take a hip-hop dance class twice a month at a studio near the campus.

Well, after listening to me, now you know about my best friend Kate and why we are such good friends. We have a lot of things in common, but we're also different in some ways, and that makes our friendship more interesting. We've been good friends for only a few years, but I'm sure we will remain friends for life. Thank you.

🔊 ▶ 7

Sophie: Good morning everyone. I'm Sophie and I am happy to speak with you today. In Nigeria, there's a saying about friendship: Hold your friends in both hands. I really like this idea, and today I'd like to tell you about my best friend. I'll tell you how we met, what we have in common, how we're different, and what we do together. After you have listened to me, you will know why I hold my friend in both hands.

🔊 ▶ 8

Sophie: Well, after listening to me, now you know about my best friend Kate and why we are such good friends. We have a lot of things in common, but we're also different in some ways, and that makes our friendship more interesting. We've been good friends for only a few years, but I'm sure we will remain friends for life. Thank you.

Unit 2 A favorite place

🔊 ▶ 9

Sophie: There's a special place I love to go because it's so quiet and peaceful. All the loud noise of the big city is gone. The air is clean, and there are lots of tall trees, colorful flowers, and birds. It also has a small, round lake in the middle with orange and white carp swimming in it. Just next to the lake, there's a narrow path going all around it, too. Sometimes, I'm the only person there, and the atmosphere is magical.

Jason: My favorite place looks kind of old fashioned, and inside it's very small and cozy. It has a few small, round wooden tables next to the window. There's this big, green, leather armchair in one corner. That's where I love to sit. Next to the armchair, there's a big, brown bookcase – around this tall – that's always full of second-hand novels. And on the walls, there are these beautiful old black-and-white photos of the city. They add a nice, old-world feeling to the place.

Emma: A favorite place of mine is bright and spacious, and also usually a little messy. There's a tall window on one wall, so I have a great view of the park across the street. On the other walls, there are a few posters of my favorite bands, and on the floor I have a yellow rug. It's not so big – maybe about this long. Actually, you can't see it very often because it's usually covered with a huge pile of my clothes, books, and stuff that comes up to about here! Yep, messy, but also comfortable.

◀))) ▶ 10

Sophie: My favorite place is a big park near my parents' house. I go there a lot to enjoy nature and fresh air in the middle of the city. I like going in the morning, when there aren't too many kids there. When I'm there, I love walking around the lake, and sometimes I bring bread from home to feed the fish. I also like to bring my camera to take pictures of the lake, especially in the rain. For me, the park is also a great place to just relax and think about things.

Jason: The Daily Grind Café is near my university. It's a great place to sit and watch people because there are all kinds of people there – students, professors, housewives, office workers, lawyers, artists – all types. I go there at least twice a week. I often go in the afternoon between classes, and I usually order a croissant. I also sometimes go in the evening to do my homework or check Facebook on my iPad. It's a lot more comfortable than the campus library.

Emma: I love my room at home, and I think it really suits my personality and style. That's important because I spend a lot of time there, especially when I just want to get away from it all and chill. I'm into gaming, so at night I play computer games on my notebook. I also have a pretty cool piano keyboard in my room, so I often put on my headphones, play some loud rock music, and use my keyboard to jam with the band. I'm in my own special world then.

◀))) ▶ 11

Ben: Hello! I'm Ben, and it's great to be here today. We all spend time in lots of different places, but I think everyone has one kind of place that feels special. For me, it's being near the sea. That's where I feel most peaceful and happy. Today, I'd like to tell you about Venice Beach in my hometown, Los Angeles. First, I'll describe what Venice Beach is like and what it has. Then, I'll tell you when I go there and what I usually do there. Finally, I'll talk about why Venice Beach is so special to me.

So, what's Venice Beach like? Well, it's *not* a quiet, romantic, tropical beach. In fact, it's a long, busy, city beach in the middle of LA. It's very popular, and on summer weekends it's always crowded with tourists, families, surfers, joggers, street musicians – all types of people. Now, let me tell you what Venice has. First of all, it has a very wide, flat, sandy beach. There's also a five-kilometer-long boardwalk next to the beach. And all along the boardwalk, there are lots of small, narrow shops right next to each other, selling sunglasses, T-shirts, handicrafts – all sorts of things.

The boardwalk also has a few tattoo studios, and there are lots of cheap food stands. You can get pizza, hot dogs, nachos, and of course, the California sushi roll! One interesting feature of Venice Beach is its open-air gym – right on the beach. Actually, it's quite famous because Arnold Schwarzenegger trained there when he was a champion bodybuilder. Lots of professional bodybuilders still train there, and tourists like to watch them.

I started going to Venice Beach about 10 years ago when I was in high school, and I still like going there with my old school friends. We go at least once a week in the summer, usually on a weekday, when it isn't so crowded. When we're there, we bodysurf, play Frisbee, and jog along the sand. Then we usually get some nachos or sushi to eat on the boardwalk. We like to stay there until around 6 p.m. because Venice is a great place to watch the sunset.

To sum up, for me, Venice Beach is the perfect place to spend a summer day, watching the people and enjoying the shops on the boardwalk, the sea, and the warm sunshine. It's special to me because when I'm there I always feel happy to be alive. Of course, Venice Beach is changing, but it's still my favorite place. I really hope you get the chance to visit Venice sometime. I'm sure you'll find it special too. Thank you.

◀))) ▶ 12

Ben: We all spend time in lots of different places, but I think everyone has one kind of place that feels special. For me, it's being near the sea. That's where I feel most peaceful and happy.

◀))) ▶ 13

Ben: Today, I'd like to tell you about Venice Beach in my hometown, Los Angeles. First, I'll describe what Venice Beach is like and what it has. Then, I'll tell you when I go there and what I usually do there. Finally, I'll talk about why Venice Beach is so special to me.

◀))) ▶ 14

Ben: To sum up, for me, Venice Beach is the perfect place to spend a summer day, watching the people and enjoying the shops on the boardwalk, the sea, and the warm sunshine. It's special to me because when I'm there I always feel happy to be alive.

◀))) ▶ 15

Ben: Of course, Venice Beach is changing, but it's still my favorite place. I really hope you get the chance to visit Venice sometime. I'm sure you'll find it special too. Thank you.

Unit 3 A prized possession

◀))) ▶ 16

Jason: Here it is – my prized possession. You can see I wear it a lot because the denim is all faded and really thin, especially here all around the top. Can you see the original dark-blue cloth here? A few months ago,

I had to put this square patch on it because there was a big hole in this pocket. Can you see it here? I think the striped green patch makes it look pretty cool and colorful. Maybe I'll put a yellow one on the other side.

Sophie: I'd like to share this very special possession with you. As you can see, it's pretty small, so it fits easily into my bag. However, it's also around an inch thick because it has 250 pages. I love the cover. Can you see? It's made of blue silk cloth, which feels really smooth. And it has a beautiful oriental design with bamboo trees and pagodas. Here, on the edge and on the corners, it's brown leather. It's difficult to see, but here on the leather there are butterflies.

Ben: This is definitely one of my favorite and most useful possessions. I love its brown, earthy colors, its rough texture, and simple design. Can you see here on the outside in the middle, there are these three cool gray round swirls on it? The size and shape are perfect too. It's not too big or too small, so it holds just the right amount for me. You can see it's wider at the top, and it has this smooth, round, thick handle that fits my fingers perfectly when I use it.

🔊 ▶ 17

Jason: I got this pair of jeans at an outlet store near my house around seven years ago. They were only 15 dollars, so I tried them on immediately. They were a little big for me, and the denim was kind of dark and stiff, but I bought them anyway. Since then, I've washed them a lot, so now the denim is soft and really comfortable. These days, I wear them just on weekends, when I hang out with friends. I know they look pretty old, but I love these jeans because they feel really natural on me.

Sophie: This diary is very special to me. In fact, it's like a best friend that knows and keeps all my secrets. It was a gift from my parents when I started high school, and now I take it with me everywhere I go. In fact, I use it almost every day to write my thoughts, create poems, and draw pictures. I think it really makes my life experiences more meaningful. A lot of the things I write in it are private, so I always keep it hidden in a safe place in my room.

Ben: I got this cup in Italy, when I was on vacation with a friend last summer. We loved hanging out in the cafés, and of course we drank a lot of great coffee there – mainly huge, milky cappuccinos. Actually, I bought this cup at our favorite small, outdoor café near our hotel in Rome. Now I keep it in my kitchen at home and use it every morning to drink my coffee. For me, this cup is the perfect souvenir because it brings back so many wonderful memories of my European summer.

🔊 ▶ 18

Grace: Good morning everyone. I'd like to begin with a simple question: What is one possession you own that you would be very sad to lose? For me, it's this pencil case. I know it doesn't look special, but it's one of my prized possessions. Today, I want to share my prized pencil case with you, so that you can understand why

it's important to me. I'll point out some of its features and tell you a little about its history and how I use it now. Finally, I'll talk about why it's important to me.

OK, I hope you can all see it clearly. Its size and shape are just normal – about the same as an airmail envelope. However, it's a lot more colorful, right? If you look closely, you can see that the outside has a striped pattern going all the way across – blue at the top, then red, blue, and yellow. Here in the middle, there's a narrow row of blue and gray triangles, and under that a row of green and yellow checks. The pencil case is made of thick cotton cloth, with this metal zipper at the top. I'm not sure if you can see clearly from there, but the zipper is a little broken at this end, so it can't close all the way: you can see it here on this slide. There's also a small hole here near the top. It's a bit faded now. The colors used to be much brighter.

So that's what it looks like. Now, can you guess how old it is? Well, I got this pencil case 15 years ago. It was a gift from my grandmother when I started elementary school. Here she is. In fact, she made it for me herself. She told me that the pencil case would always help me get good grades in school. I kept it in my backpack all through elementary, junior high, and high school – until the zipper broke!

Now I keep it on my desk at home, and I always have around 20 pens and pencils in it. Of course, these days, I do most of my schoolwork on my computer, but I still like to use my pens and pencils when I brainstorm, write notes, make lists – things like that.

In conclusion, I hope you now understand why this useful, but old and faded, cloth pencil case is one of my prized possessions. It's not because it's beautiful or expensive. It's because it brings back childhood memories. It's because someone very special to me made it with her own hands. Most of all, it's because my grandmother gave it to me. Thank you.

🔊 ▶ 19

Grace: Good morning everyone. I'd like to begin with a simple question: What is one possession you own that you would be very sad to lose? For me, it's this pencil case. I know it doesn't look special, but it's one of my prized possessions.

🔊 ▶ 20

Grace: Today, I want to share my prized pencil case with you, so that you can understand why it's important to me. I'll point out some of its features and tell you a little about its history and how I use it now. Finally, I'll talk about why it's important to me.

🔊 ▶ 21

Grace: In conclusion, I hope you now understand why this useful, but old and faded, cloth pencil case is one of my prized possessions.

🔊 ▶ 22

Grace: It's not because it's beautiful or expensive. It's because it brings back childhood memories. It's because someone very special to me made it with her own hands. Most of all, it's because my grandmother gave it to me. Thank you.

Unit 4 A memorable experience

🔊 ▶ 23

Grace: This experience happened to me a few years ago, and it was the first time I met someone famous. One day, my best friend Donna and I were at a trendy diner called Johnny's for lunch. We were sitting at the counter, just eating our burgers and fries and talking about our classes at school, when the lead singer of our favorite rock band walked in! It was Jack Thomas from the Outsiders. We couldn't believe it. It was so amazing!

Ben: It was when I was 15 that I got my very first summer job at a golf course driving range near my house. In fact, my dad often played golf there, and he knew the manager, George Olsen. So, Mr. Olsen agreed to hire me to work four days a week. He said I could start work the next day at 9 a.m. I remember that morning when I rode my bicycle to the golf course. I was pretty nervous because it was my first job, but I was also really thrilled to earn my own money.

Sophie: I had this experience during my second year of junior high school, when I was 14. I did a one-month homestay in Spain. To be honest, I didn't really want to go because I was worried about leaving my family and friends for a whole month. It seemed like such a long time. It was also very scary to be so far from home on my own for the first time – especially in a different culture with people who expect me to speak and understand Spanish.

🔊 ▶ 24

Grace: At first, we both just stared at him. Then he walked towards us, smiled, and sat next to me. He ordered his food, and then after a couple of minutes he started talking to us. He asked us about our school, our interests, and the kind of music we like. We talked to him for a few minutes. Finally, when he was leaving, he gave us tickets for that night's concert! He seemed like such a nice, normal person. It changed my view of rock stars.

Ben: I guess I looked nervous, so Mr. Olsen encouraged me a lot. First of all, he showed me around the course and explained about my duties. Then, he said, "Now it's time to start work. I hope you enjoy the job." Soon after that, I walked around the driving range with a big cart and collected the balls from the ground. Then I washed them and put them in baskets for the golfers. I did that five times. When I finished at 5 o'clock, I was totally exhausted, but happy.

Sophie: In the beginning, it was really confusing because the customs were so different, and I couldn't understand what people were saying. And then I got really frustrated because I couldn't communicate much in Spanish. However, little by little, I began to understand more and was able to have more interesting conversations with my host family. In the

end, I learned so much and made a lot of new friends. I didn't want to go home!

🔊 ▶ 25

Patrick: Hello everyone. A tropical island, my dad, the sea, a turtle, a test. What do these things have in common? Well, they were all part of one of the most memorable experiences I've had in my life. Today, I'd like to tell you about that experience. I'll describe what happened and how I felt and explain why that experience is so memorable to me now.

It happened when I was 14. I was on a vacation with my parents on the island of Maui. My dad's a diver, and he loves the sea. So one day, he asked me if I wanted to try scuba diving. At first, I said no because it seemed scary. My dad just said, "That's OK, but I really hope we can go diving together someday." When he said that, I decided to try it.

I started my diving course the next morning. To begin with, I watched a video about diving safety, and then we went into the pool to practice basic skills. I had trouble with some of them, but my instructor, Mi Young, kept encouraging me. After lunch, I did my first dive in the sea. It was absolutely terrifying! When we first got into the water, my heart was pounding. I was scared the whole time. I didn't enjoy it, and I wanted to quit, but Mi Young said, "Don't worry, tomorrow will be better."

The next day, I did my second dive. I was still uneasy at first, but after a while I began to feel more comfortable underwater. Then something wonderful happened. We were near a coral reef with lots of fish, and suddenly I saw a huge green turtle swimming next to me. It was so awesome! After that, I completely forgot my fear, and I began to notice the amazing underwater world.

On the last day, I passed my final test and finished the course. Mi Young smiled and said, "Congratulations, you're now a diver!" And my dad said, "Way to go, son. I'm very proud of you." I was also proud of myself because it was challenging and I didn't give up. And I was really excited about diving with my dad.

So, in closing, I can say that my diving adventure was definitely an experience to remember. It helped me gain more confidence in myself, and it taught me appreciation for our beautiful underwater world. Most of all, it gave me a fun, interesting hobby I can share with my dad. Now, I hope hearing about my memorable experience encourages you to share yours. Thank you.

🔊 ▶ 26

Patrick: Hello everyone. A tropical island, my dad, the sea, a turtle, a test. What do these things have in common? Well, they were all part of one of the most memorable experiences I've had in my life.

🔊 ▶ 27

Patrick: Today, I'd like to tell you about that experience. I'll describe what happened and how I felt, and explain why that experience is so memorable to me now.

Patrick: So, in closing, I can say that my diving adventure was definitely an experience to remember.

Patrick: It helped me gain more confidence in myself, and it taught me appreciation for our beautiful underwater world. Most of all, it gave me a fun, interesting hobby I can share with my dad.

Patrick: Now, I hope hearing about my memorable experience encourages you to share yours. Thank you.

Sophie (Versions 1–3): I had this experience during my second year of junior high school, when I was 14. I did a one-month homestay in Spain. To be honest, I didn't really want to go because I was worried about leaving my family and friends for a whole month. It seemed like such a long time.

Ben: I was also really thrilled to earn my own money.

Grace: We couldn't believe it. It was so amazing.

Ben: When I finished at 5 o'clock I was totally exhausted, but happy.

Patrick: After that, I completely forgot my fear.

Sophie: It was also very scary to be so far from home.

Patrick: It was absolutely terrifying!

Unit 5 I'll show you how

33

Patrick: Hello. I'm glad you all could make it today. I know you're all busy students, and most of you don't have much time to cook and eat big meals. That means you need lots of snacks to keep up your energy and concentration when you're studying. So today, I'm going to show you how to make a quick, easy, delicious, and healthy snack. It will give you enough energy to write a report or study for an exam.

Grace: Hi everyone. Thanks for coming today. You know, it's a fact that 70 percent of people in their 20s want to lose weight and be fitter. However, most students don't have the time or money to join an expensive fitness club. Well, don't worry! Today, I'm going to teach you how to do a very simple, but effective, exercise that you can do on your own at home. It will help you to look slim with a strong, flat stomach. I promise!

Ben: Hello everyone. Tell me, would you like to be able to prepare a special birthday lunch for your sweetheart? How about a lovely Mother's Day breakfast for your mom? Yes, me too. Are you a good cook? No, I'm not either. But that's not a problem because I'm going to show you a simple way to make a heart-shaped egg. It'll make that birthday or Mother's Day meal special – without a lot of fancy cooking!

Sophie: I often have a hard time thinking of fun, inexpensive birthday or holiday gifts for friends and family. So I searched on the Internet and found a very cool idea. It's how to make colorful paper fortune cookies. I recently made some for my friend at Chinese New Year, and she loved them. So today, I'd like to teach you. It's the perfect homemade gift to impress your friends with your creativity and your English!

34

Patrick: All right. Let's get started. This snack is a Mexican dip called guacamole. For this, you should have two avocados. Remember to buy ones that aren't too hard. You also need a small onion, a large ripe tomato, one tablespoon of lemon juice, and a pinch of salt. Finally, for dipping, I recommend carrot and cucumber sticks as they're crunchy and also healthy.

Grace: Are you ready? OK. Before you begin, you should put on comfortable, loose clothing so you can move your legs easily. You also need a chair to hold on to. Please make sure you use a chair without arms. That's important. Finally, you need a small pillow to put between your knees. If you don't have a pillow, no problem, you can use a rolled-up towel.

Ben: Right, here's what you need to begin. First of all, one hard-boiled egg. It should be freshly cooked and peeled. You also need a clean, empty milk carton or juice carton and one round chopstick. It works better if you use a round chopstick, not one with square edges. And finally, you'll need two rubber bands. Normal, medium-size bands will work fine.

Sophie: OK. Before you start, you need a sheet of colorful gift-wrap paper. Make sure it's not too thin. You also need a round dish for drawing a circle on the paper. It should be around 10 centimeters across. In addition, you need a pair of scissors, a pencil, and a glue stick. Finally, you need some small, narrow slips of paper for the fortune inside the cookie. Small Post-its work fine.

Ben: OK. Here's how we do it. Boil the egg for 10 minutes and peel it completely. Use the scissors to cut one side of the milk carton into a rectangle that's 20 centimeters long and 8 centimeters wide. Make sure that the short side is not wider than 8 centimeters. Then, fold along the middle of the long side of the rectangle so it makes a V shape, like this. Put the peeled egg in the center of the carton, like this. After that, lay the chopstick on the top of the egg and press down gently. Be careful not to press down too hard, or the egg will break. Now, use the rubber bands and tie each end of the chopstick and carton together to hold the egg inside. See? Are there any questions? OK. Be sure to keep the rubber bands in place at least 10 minutes. Then remove the chopstick and the rubber bands. And this is what it looks like. Finally, cut the egg in half with a sharp knife. It's important to use a sharp knife. See? What a lovely yellow and white heart!

Emma: Good afternoon everyone. Thanks for coming. Tell me, are you concerned about all the plastic we use that's hurting the environment? Do you buy re-sealable bags to keep food fresh and dry? Do you find them expensive and troublesome to reuse? Well, don't worry because today I'm going to teach you how to make your own airtight re-sealable bag in just six easy steps. You'll be able to keep things fresh, and you'll save money because you won't need to buy any more expensive re-sealable bags.

OK. Here's what you need to start. Actually, it's just a few things. First, you need the item you want to keep dry, like an opened bag of rice, flour, or sugar. You also need a plastic bottle with a screw-on top. A medium-sized water bottle works perfectly. Also, you'll need a pair of scissors or a sharp kitchen knife. And finally, a kitchen towel.

So, let's see how to make the container. To begin with, unscrew the top from the plastic bottle. Make sure you keep the top because you'll need it in a few minutes. OK. Next, use the scissors or knife to cut all around the plastic bottle, about 4 to 5 centimeters from the top. You should try to cut in a straight line, so there are no sharp, uneven edges. Here, like this. Right. Then, wash and dry the top of the bottle and the screw top. You don't need the rest. It's important to make sure the section of the bottle and the screw top are both clean and completely dry. OK. Now, twist the top of the open food bag and push it through the section of the bottle so that it comes out the top. Make sure you have about 5 or 6 centimeters of the bag above the section of the bottle. About this much, see? Is that part clear? Good. Then, fold the bag all the way down over the top of the section of the bottle, like this. Be sure to hold it flat on the bottle with your hand. OK, we're almost finished. Finally, screw the top back onto the bottle over the bag. Remember to screw the top on tightly. And now your container is ready to use.

So that's how to make a simple, reusable storage container to keep everything fresh, save money, and recycle your plastic bottles. As you saw, you don't need a lot of materials, and the six steps only take a few minutes. Just keep in mind the few key points I mentioned, and you'll have no trouble. I encourage you to try it for yourself at home and stop buying all those re-sealable bags. Thank you.

Emma: Good afternoon everyone. Thanks for coming. Tell me, are you concerned about all the plastic we use that's hurting the environment? Do you buy re-sealable bags to keep food fresh and dry? Do you find them expensive and troublesome to reuse?

Emma: Well, don't worry because today I'm going to teach you how to make your own airtight re-sealable bag in just six easy steps. You'll be able to keep things fresh, and you'll save money because you won't need to buy any more expensive re-sealable bags.

Emma: So, that's how to make a simple, reusable storage container to keep everything fresh, save money, and recycle your plastic bottles.

Emma: As you saw, you don't need a lot of materials, and the six steps only take a few minutes. Just keep in mind the few key points I mentioned, and you'll have no trouble.

Emma: I encourage you to try it for yourself at home and stop buying all those re-sealable bags. Thank you.

Emma: OK. Now, twist the top of the open food bag and push it through the section of the bottle so that it comes out the top. Make sure you have about 5 or 6 centimeters of the bag above the section of the bottle. About this much, see? Is that part clear?

Ben: After that, lay the chopstick on the top of the egg and press down gently. Be careful not to press down too hard, or the egg will break. Now, use the rubber bands and tie each end of the chopstick and carton together to hold the egg inside. See? Are there any questions?

Unit 6 Screen magic

Emma: *Life of Pi* is a magical adventure movie about an Indian boy named Pi who spends months on a small boat in the ocean with a Bengal tiger. The film begins when Pi is an adult, telling an interviewer about his childhood in India, where his father owned a zoo. Pi's family leave India with their animals on a boat to Canada, but a storm sinks the boat, and all of Pi's family die. Pi escapes in a lifeboat with four animals, including the tiger. The tiger kills the other animals, but Pi and the tiger eventually learn to accept each other.

Patrick: *The Walking Dead* is a horror drama series that takes place in America in the near future. The main character is Rick Grimes, a sheriff who wakes up after being in a coma for several months and discovers that zombies have taken over the world. He goes to Atlanta to search for his wife and son and narrowly escapes the zombies. Rick then meets another survivor, and they go to a camp, where Rick finds his wife and son and other survivors. Together, they fight against the zombies and also against other groups of survivors, who will do anything to stay alive.

Grace: *The Hunger Games* is the first of several sci-fi adventure movies based on a popular novel. It's set in the future in the nation of Panem. Every year, the

Capitol of Panem chooses a teenage boy and girl from each of the 12 districts to compete in the Hunger Games – a televised fight to the death. The film centers on 16-year-old Katniss Everdeen from District 12, who volunteers for the Hunger Games instead of her younger sister. Katniss goes to the Capitol with a boy named Peeta to get training before the games begin. Then, Katniss must enter the arena to fight for her life.

Ben: *Game of Thrones* is a fantasy drama series that is set on the fictional continent of Westeros. There are lots of characters in the series, and the plot includes three connected storylines. One follows the members of seven noble families, who are fighting for control of the Iron Throne. The second storyline is about the threat of a long, freezing winter and monsters from the north. Finally, the third storyline focuses on the former rulers of Westeros, who want to take back the kingdom they lost.

◀) ▶ 45

Emma: The cinematography in *Life of Pi* is fantastic. Many scenes are like beautiful photographs, for example, when a whale leaps up through water full of glowing jellyfish. Then there's the special effects to create the tiger. They're spectacular and very realistic. Most of the time, I totally believed that the tiger was a hundred percent real. I suppose the only thing I didn't like so much was the story itself. It was kind of slow moving and also a little confusing. I wanted more action. And at the end, I wanted to know what really happened in the lifeboat.

Patrick: I'm not a fan of horror, and *The Walking Dead* doesn't change my mind. First of all, the plot is ridiculous and pretty unoriginal. You know, somebody wakes up and discovers that zombies have taken over the world: it's been done many times. And most of the actors who play the zombies are terrible. Their actions and movements are so unnatural. And the dialogue is unrealistic. The things that the survivors say to each other are often unbelievable. It's hard to imagine real people saying that.

Grace: I loved *The Hunger Games* novels, and I think the movie is even better. First of all, the actors' performances are excellent – especially Jennifer Lawrence, who plays Katniss. She makes the main character seem very real and believable. The movie also cuts some of the scenes in the book, so the story has more action and is faster moving. That makes it more exciting, I think. The one feature of the movie I found disappointing was the cinematography: it's really irritating. In many scenes, the camera is shaking in order to make the action seem more realistic, but it doesn't really work well.

Ben: I'm not into fantasy, but the *Game of Thrones* is an awesome series. The plot, with its three stories, is a little complicated, but fascinating. And the acting is fantastic. The actors really bring all the colorful characters alive – especially Sean Bean, who plays the main character of Eddard Stark in Season 1. The cinematography is also stunning, with

amazing scenery of the medieval castles, palaces, and landscapes. The only thing I don't like so much about *Game of Thrones* is the violence. There's a lot of fighting and blood. But all in all, I'm really into it.

◀) ▶ 46

Jason: Hello everyone. Here's a movie quiz question for you. When was the first Superman movie made? Does anyone know the answer? It was in 1951. And it may surprise you that more than 10 Superman movies have been made. The one I want to talk about today is *Man of Steel*, which was released in 2013. It's an action movie directed by Zack Snyder, and it stars Henry Cavill as Superman and Russell Crowe as his father, Jor-El.

Man of Steel is set on the planet Krypton and on Earth, including the United States and Canada. The movie covers Superman's life from infancy to his 30s. The movie tells the story of Superman's origins – how he becomes Superman. At the beginning, Krypton is dying, so its leader, Jor-El, sends his baby son, Kal-El, to Earth. Kal-El is adopted by kindly farmers in Kansas, and they name him Clark.

As a child, Clark discovers that he has special powers, and later he tries to find out where he comes from. In his travels, he meets the reporter Lois Lane, and he communicates by hologram with his father, Jor-El. Clark learns that he was sent to Earth to bring hope to mankind. Meanwhile, the evil General Zod from Krypton wants to destroy the human race. Clark finally realizes he must become Superman to protect the people on Earth from their powerful enemies.

Man of Steel is different from other Superman movies, and there are a lot of things I liked about it. First, the plot is easy to follow, without confusing flashbacks. As well, the visual effects are absolutely spectacular! The battle between Superman and Zod is awesome. Finally, the acting is excellent. Henry Cavill does a great job playing Clark Kent as he struggles to find his life purpose. He's also a very believable superhero. Russell Crowe also gives a moving performance as Jor-El.

So is there anything I didn't like about *Man of Steel*? Well, yes. I think the dialogue is too serious: there's not enough humor in this movie. I also think the ending is a little disappointing, especially after all the amazing action scenes. But if you haven't seen it yet, don't worry, I won't tell you how it ends!

So what's my final rating of *Man of Steel*? Overall, I'd give it four stars out of five for its interesting plot, fantastic special effects, awesome action scenes, and great cast. It's definitely worth seeing, and I recommend you see it on a big screen in 3-D – with popcorn! Thank you.

◀) ▶ 47

Jason: Hello everyone. Here's a movie quiz question for you. When was the first Superman movie made? Does anyone know the answer? It was in 1951. And it may surprise you that more than 10 Superman movies have been made.

🔊 ▶ 48

Jason: The one I want to talk about today is *Man of Steel*, which was released in 2013. It's an action movie directed by Zack Snyder, and it stars Henry Cavill as Superman and Russell Crowe as his father, Jor-El.

🔊 ▶ 49

Jason: So, what's my final rating of *Man of Steel*?

🔊 ▶ 50

Jason: Overall, I'd give it four stars out of five for its interesting plot, fantastic special effects, awesome action scenes, and great cast.

🔊 ▶ 51

Jason: It's definitely worth seeing, and I recommend you see it on a big screen in 3D – with popcorn! Thank you.

🔊 ▶ 52

Emma: After seven years as a prisoner in Iraq, Brody is rescued and returns to the United States as a war hero.

Patrick: It takes place in Tokyo during the rainy season, and it's the story of 15-year-old Takao, who dreams of becoming a shoemaker.

Grace: Brad Pitt plays a United Nations official, who travels all over the world, trying to stop zombies from infecting everyone.

Ben: It stars Sandra Bullock and George Clooney as astronauts on the space shuttle *Explorer*, which is damaged while they're on a mission in outer space.

Unit 1 Expansion activities

▶ 1

Ben: Hello everyone, I'm Ben. Welcome to the Expansion activities for Unit 1. Let's first look at the different parts of introductions and conclusions. Watch these introductions by Patrick, Emma, and Jason.

Patrick: Good morning. Today, I want to tell you about my best friend, Nick. I'll explain how we met, what we have in common, how we're different, and finally, what we do together.

Emma: Hello everyone. There's a very old saying about friendship that I really like: "Friendship is one mind in two bodies." Today, I'd like to tell you about my best friend, Hana. We only met a year ago at our part-time job, but we already feel like sisters.

Jason: A common saying about friends is, "A friend in need is a friend indeed." My talk will include how I met Sami, how we're similar and different, and what kind of things we do when we hang out together.

▶ 2

Ben: Did you notice what was missing from each speaker's introduction? Patrick didn't have an opener to get the audience's attention; Emma didn't include a

preview to let her audience know what the main points will be in her presentation; and Jason left out the topic statement. Now let's watch their conclusions.

Patrick: Nick and I have a lot in common, but we also have some differences that make our friendship interesting. And I think our friendship will last a long time. Thank you.

Emma: To sum up, Hana and I have known each other for only a short time, but we have a lot in common and feel very close. Thank you for listening.

Jason: So now you know a lot about Sami and why I think he's such a good friend to me. Even though we are different in some ways, I really think that we'll be friends for life. That's all.

▶ 3

Ben: Did you notice what was missing from each speaker's conclusion? Patrick didn't use a signal phrase to let the audience know he was starting his conclusion; Emma didn't include a memorable closer to end her presentation; and Jason forgot to thank the audience at the end. Remember that all these parts of the introduction and conclusion are important. They will make your presentation clear, interesting, and memorable for the audience.

▶ 4

Ben: Now let's look at the different types of openers and closers you can use to begin and end presentations. Here they are again. Now watch Patrick, Emma, and Jason. Notice what type of opener each speaker uses.

Patrick: Good afternoon everyone, I'm Patrick. Last year was a difficult time for me. My girlfriend broke up with me, I failed an entrance exam, and I injured my leg in football practice. Actually, I was miserable for a long time, and I wasn't fun to be with. However, my best friend Nick was always there for me. Today, I want to . . .

Emma: Good morning. What is one thing in your life that you can't live without? Well, for me it's my friends. Today, I . . .

Jason: Hello everyone. Here's an interesting fact you may not know: Every year on the first Sunday in August, there's a holiday called Friendship Day. That's right, it's for us to be thankful for our friends. This morning, I'd like to . . .

▶ 5

Ben: Did you notice that Patrick told a short story, Emma asked the audience a question, and Jason began with an interesting fact? These are all good ways to quickly get the audience interested in your topic. OK, let's now look at the same speakers ending their presentations. Notice what type of closer each speaker uses.

Patrick: So, after you go home today, think about what it means to be a good friend and make sure you do something nice for your friends soon. Thank you for listening.

Emma: In the end, when I think about the meaning of friendship, I realize that friends are really what makes life worth living. Thank you.

Jason: I hope that hearing about my friendship with Sami has motivated you to tell us about your best friend too. I'm looking forward to that. Thank you.

 6

Ben: Did you notice that Patrick gave the audience a call to action by asking them to do something after they go home? Emma ended by emphasizing the importance of her topic, and Jason finished by passing the mike to other speakers. These are all good ways to make your presentation memorable.

 7

Ben: In Unit 1, you learned how to make and use effective note cards. Did you make two note cards for Patrick's presentation about his friend Nick? Are they similar to Patrick's note cards on page 92? Notice that Patrick's note cards follow the tips from Unit 1 on page 16. Do your note cards follow the tips? Now, watch Patrick giving his presentation and notice how he uses his note cards. As you watch try to answer these three questions.

Patrick: I've known Nick since junior high school and he's one of my best friends. What kind of person is he? Well, I guess you can say he's pretty quiet and serious – exactly the opposite of me. He likes spending a lot of time at home with his music and he's not really into parties or hanging out. He's also not very neat and tidy. In fact, his room is a real mess – the floor is covered with his clothes. It kind of looks like a typhoon hit his room! Nick's totally into classical music, and he loves playing the piano – usually two or three hours a day. I don't really enjoy classical music, but I'm a big fan of blues music.

 8

Ben: I'm sure you noticed that Patrick uses his note cards very effectively when he's speaking. He only looks at them a few times, he holds them comfortably, and he doesn't read out loud while looking down at them. Using note cards effectively, like Patrick, takes practice. So don't worry, you'll get much better at it during this course.

 9

Ben: Making good eye contact is one of the most important presentation techniques. It helps you connect with your audience and helps your audience connect with you. First, let's see some examples of what not to do. Watch Patrick, Emma, and Jason and notice what each speaker is doing wrong.

Patrick: Nick's totally into classical music, and he loves playing the piano – usually two or three hours a day. I don't really enjoy classical music, but I'm a big fan of blues music. So, when Nick and I meet up, around once a month, I usually take him to one of my favorite live blues clubs. Actually, I think he's starting to like blues. Occasionally, I go with him to a classical

concert in the city, but I always fall asleep in the middle of it!

Emma: Hana and I both love singing karaoke and going out to eat, especially to restaurants we've never tried before. That's what we often do on Saturdays. We go out for dinner, then sing karaoke for a couple of hours. Hana likes Italian food and I love Thai food, so we take turns choosing a different restaurant each time.

Jason: Sami loves trying new things – especially extreme sports. Right now, he's into paragliding and kite surfing. That's a bit too much for me. I prefer running, cycling, and swimming. They're a lot safer and really good exercise. Actually, Sami and I are training together for a triathlon race. That's what we do twice a week, on Wednesday evening and Sunday afternoon.

 10

Ben: Did you notice that all three speakers had problems with eye contact? Patrick didn't look at the audience enough, and he also hid his face a few times with his note card. Emma *did* make eye contact, but she moved her eyes back and forth too fast and too evenly, like a lighthouse. And Jason looked for too long at only two or three people. That can make the audience members uncomfortable. Now watch Sophie and notice how she follows the eye contact tips effectively.

Sophie: So, how would I describe Kate? Well, she's very easygoing and laid-back – just like me! We don't get upset very often, and we don't argue much. We're also both very positive, optimistic people. Our number one passion is hip-hop music and fashion. You can guess that when you see us because we both always dress in street style clothes.

 11

Ben: Sophie made eye contact very effectively, didn't she? She looked at everyone in the audience during her presentation. That helped them become more involved and interested in what she was saying. Remember, the more you practice, the easier it will be for you to use good eye contact to make your presentations better.

 12

Ben: You can use PowerPoint to add a visual element to your presentation. Try to follow the tips in the *Present yourself!* section of every unit. They will help you to use PowerPoint more effectively so your audience can enjoy your presentation more. Now watch two versions of Patrick giving the same presentation.

Patrick (Version 1): Nick's totally into classical music, and he loves playing the piano – usually two or three hours a day. I don't really enjoy classical music, but I'm a big fan of blues music. So, when Nick and I meet up, around once a month, I usually take him to one of my favorite live blues clubs. Actually, I think he's starting to like blues. Occasionally, I go with him to a classical concert in the city, but I always fall asleep in the middle of it!

Patrick (Version 2): Nick's totally into classical music, and he loves playing the piano – usually two or three hours a day. I don't really enjoy classical music, but I'm a big fan of blues music. So, when Nick and I meet up, around once a month, I usually take him to one of my favorite live blues clubs. Actually, I think he's starting to like blues. Occasionally, I go with him to a classical concert in the city, but I always fall asleep in the middle of it!

 13

Ben: Patrick's second version was much better, wasn't it? In his first version, he had too much information on the slide, and he used complete sentences. But in the second version, Patrick used keywords and short phrases on his slide. Remember those simple tips whenever you use PowerPoint.

Unit 2 Expansion activities

 14

Grace: Hi, I'm Grace. In Unit 1, we looked at different types of openers and closers. Here's some more practice to help you use them in your presentations. Watch Sophie, Jason, and Emma begin their presentations about their favorite places. What kind of opener do they each use? Before you watch, look again at the openers on page 15.

Sophie: Good morning everyone. Do you have a favorite place where you love to spend time? There's a special place I love to go because it's so quiet and peaceful. All the loud noise of the big city is gone. The air is clean, and there are lots of tall trees, colorful flowers, and birds.

Jason: Hello everyone. You're probably not aware of this, but there are more than 21,000 cafés in this country. That's right, 21,000! And one of them, which is near my home, is my favorite place. My favorite place looks kind of old fashioned, and inside it's very small and cozy.

Emma: Good afternoon. There's a famous quote from the classic film *The Wizard of Oz*, "There's no place like home." I think that's really true. A favorite place of mine is bright and spacious and also usually a little messy. I think it really suits my personality and style.

 15

Grace: Did you notice that each speaker used a different type of opener? Sophie began with a question, Jason used an interesting fact about cafés, and Emma opened with a saying. So, which opener did you like best? Now watch the end of their presentations to see what type of closer they each use. Before you watch, look again at the closers on page 15.

Sophie: For me, the park is also a great place to just relax and think about things. To sum up, the park

always helps me let go of stress and worry and calms my mind. That's why it's so important to me.

Jason: So now you know all about my favorite café. It really is a great place, and if you have the chance to drop by one day, please do. I'm positive you'll find it special too.

Emma: All in all, I really feel like I'm in my own world when I'm in my room. So now that I've told you all about my favorite place, I hope you feel motivated to share your special place.

 16

Grace: Did you notice that each speaker used a different type of closer? Sophie emphasized how special the park is to her, and Jason's closer was an invitation for the audience to visit his favorite café. Finally, Emma ended by "passing the mike" – suggesting that others talk about their favorite places. Which closer did you like best?

 17

Grace: In the **Developing presentation techniques** section of Unit 2, you learned about making gestures for descriptions. Watch this example from Emma to see how she uses gestures when she describes her favorite place.

Emma: There's a tall window on one wall, so I have a great view of the park across the street. On the other walls, there are a few posters of my favorite bands, and on the floor, I have a yellow rug. It's not so big, maybe about this long. Actually, you can't see it very often because it's usually covered with a huge pile of my clothes, books, and stuff that comes up to about here!

 18

Grace: Did Emma's gestures emphasize the words you underlined? First, she showed how long her rug was. Then she emphasized how big her pile of clothes and things was: it comes up to here. Now let's see how Ben uses gestures when he's describing Venice Beach.

Ben: Now, let me tell you what Venice has. First of all, it has a very wide flat, sandy beach; there's also a five-kilometer-long boardwalk next to the beach. And all along the boardwalk, there are lots of small, narrow shops, right next to each other, selling sunglasses, T-shirts, handicrafts – all sorts of things.

 19

Grace: Ben used a gesture to show that the beach is very wide. Then he used his hands again to emphasize that the shops on the boardwalk are narrow and close to each other. Remember that using gestures can help the audience imagine what you're describing.

 20

Grace: In Unit 2, you also learned about effective body language and posture when you're presenting. Watch Sophie and Jason. Notice what they're doing wrong.

Sophie: My favorite place is a big park near my parents' house. I go there a lot to enjoy nature and fresh air in the middle of the city. I like going in the morning, when there aren't too many kids there. When I'm there, I love walking around the lake, and sometimes I bring bread from home to feed the fish. I also like to bring my camera to take pictures of the lake, especially in the rain. For me, the park is also a great place to just relax and think about things.

Jason: The Daily Grind Café is near my university. It's a great place to sit and watch people because there's all kinds of people there – students, professors, housewives, office workers, lawyers, artists – all types. I often go in the afternoon between classes, and I usually order a croissant. I also sometimes go in the evening to do homework or check Facebook on my iPad. It's a lot more comfortable than the campus library.

 21

Grace: Sophie and Jason each had problems with their body language and posture. Sophie didn't smile and stood too straight with her feet too close together and stiff arms. She also played with her hair and touched her face because she was nervous. Jason had the opposite problem: he looked too casual. He leaned against the table, and he crossed his arms in front of his chest. He also put his hands in his pockets, trying to show his confidence. Now look at Ben and notice his body language and posture.

Ben: I started going to Venice Beach about 10 years ago, when I was in high school, and I still like going there with my old school friends. We go at least once a week in the summer, usually on a weekday, when it isn't so crowded. When we're there, we bodysurf, play Frisbee, and jog along the sand. Then we usually get some nachos or sushi to eat on the boardwalk. We like to stay there until around 6 p.m. because Venice is a great place to watch the sunset.

 22

Grace: Ben's body language and posture were much more effective because he followed all the Dos and Don'ts on page 29. And I'm sure that helped the audience enjoy his presentation.

 23

Grace: You may decide to use PowerPoint for your presentation, so let's focus on the tips in the **Present yourself!** section. Watch two versions of Ben giving his presentation. Notice what he is doing right and wrong in each one.

Ben (Version 1): So, what's Venice Beach like? Well, it's *not* a quiet, romantic, tropical beach. In fact, it's a long, busy, city beach in the middle of LA. It's very popular, and on summer weekends it's always crowded with tourists, families, surfers, joggers, street musicians – all types of people. Now, first let me tell you what Venice has. First of all, it has a very wide flat, sandy beach. There's also a five-kilometer-long boardwalk next to the beach. And all along the boardwalk, there are lots of small, narrow shops, right next to each other, selling sunglasses, T-shirts, handicrafts – all sorts of things.

Ben (Version 2): So, what's Venice Beach like? Well, it's *not* a quiet, romantic, tropical beach. In fact, it's a long, busy, city beach in the middle of LA. It's very popular, and on summer weekends it's always crowded with tourists, families, surfers, joggers, street musicians – all types of people. Now, let me tell you what Venice has. First of all, it has a very wide, flat, sandy beach. There's also a five-kilometer-long boardwalk next to the beach. And all along the boardwalk, there's lots of small, narrow shops, right next to each other, selling sunglasses, T-shirts, handicrafts – all sorts of things.

 24

Grace: Ben's first version wasn't very good. He stood in front of the screen, blocking the view of his slides. He also turned his back to the audience while he was talking. However, Ben's second version was much better. He stood to one side of the screen so everyone could see. He also kept his body facing the audience while he was speaking. Remember these two PowerPoint tips, and you'll quickly become an effective speaker.

Unit 3 Expansion activities

 25

Patrick: Hi everyone, I'm Patrick. I'll be your guide today. Let's begin by watching Jason, Sophie, and Ben introduce their prized possessions. Notice the type of opener they each use. Before you watch, look again at the openers on page 15.

Jason: Good morning everyone. Big, small, old, new, expensive, cheap, practical, useless, valuable, worthless. These words describe the things we own: our possessions. Today, I want to tell you about . . .

Sophie: Good morning everyone. I'd like to begin with a simple question: What is one possession you own that you would be very sad to lose? For me, it's this diary. I know it doesn't look special, but it's one of my prized possessions. Today, I want to . . .

Ben: Hi. I'm Ben, and I'm pleased to be here today. We all own many things in our life, but for most people, only a very few of our possessions are truly special or meaningful to us. This morning, I want to share . . .

 26

Patrick: Did you notice what kind of opener they each used? Jason began with a mystery list of adjectives for possessions. Sophie asked the audience a question to think about. And Ben opened with a general statement about people and possessions. Now watch their conclusions and see what type of closer they each use.

Jason: To conclude, I'm sure you can now see why this old, inexpensive, faded pair of jeans is very special to me. I'm sure you have precious possessions like these jeans that mean a lot to you, too. Keep them, value them, and remember they are part of who you are.

Sophie: To sum up, this small, inexpensive, plain-looking diary that I carry around with me everywhere is very valuable to me. It's not only because I enjoy writing about my daily activities in it. Most of all, it's because the pages of my diary contain my thoughts and my dreams.

Ben: All in all, for me, this cup is the perfect souvenir because it brings back so many wonderful memories of my European summer. I'm sure that I'll take it with me and use it every day, wherever I live in the future.

▶ 27

Patrick: They each ended in a different way, right? Jason ended with a call to action. He told the audience to keep and value their prized possessions. Sophie emphasized the importance of her prized possession. Finally, Ben's closer was a thought about the future. So, which closer will work best for your prized possession?

▶ 28

Patrick: In this unit's **Developing presentation techniques** section, you learned that a presentation about a prized possession is like a show-and-tell. Now watch two versions of Grace talking about her pencil case to see the show-and-tell tips in action.

Grace (Version 1): OK, I hope you can all see it clearly. Its size and shape are just normal – about the same as an airmail envelope. However, it's a lot more colorful, right? If you look closely, you can see that the outside has a striped pattern going all the way across – blue at the top, then red, blue, and yellow. Here in the middle, there's a narrow row of blue and gray triangles, and under that a row of green and yellow checks. The pencil case is made of thick cotton cloth, with this metal zipper at the top. I'm not sure if you can see clearly from there, but the zipper is a little broken at this end, so it can't close all the way – you can see it here on this slide.

Grace (Version 2): OK, I hope you can all see it clearly. Its size and shape are just normal – about the same as an airmail envelope. However, it's a lot more colorful, right? If you look closely, you can see that the outside has a striped pattern going all the way across – blue at the top, then red, blue and yellow. Here in the middle, there's a narrow row of blue and gray triangles, and under that a row of green and yellow checks. The pencil case is made of thick cotton cloth, with this metal zipper at the top. I'm not sure if you can see clearly from there, but the zipper is a little broken at this end, so it can't close all the way – you can see it here on this slide.

▶ 29

Patrick: Grace's first version wasn't very good. She held the pencil case in front of her face, and she waved it around. Also, she didn't turn it around to highlight its special features. Finally, her slide didn't help because the photo was too small. Now, Grace's second version was better because she followed the show-and-tell tips. She held the pencil case up long enough for everyone to see. She didn't wave it around, and she pointed out its special features. Finally, her photo of the pencil case was big enough for us to easily see the features.

▶ 30

Patrick: You can also help the audience notice interesting features of an object with the expressions you use. Watch this section of Grace's presentation. Notice the show-and-tell expressions she uses when she describes her pencil case.

Grace: OK, I hope you can all see it clearly. Its size and shape are just normal – about the same as an airmail envelope. However, it's a lot more colorful, right? If you look closely, you can see that the outside has a striped pattern going all the way across – blue at the top, then red, blue, and yellow. Here in the middle, there's a narrow row of blue and gray triangles, and under that a row of green and yellow checks. The pencil case is made of thick cotton cloth, with this metal zipper at the top. I'm not sure if you can see clearly from there, but the zipper is a little broken at this end, so it can't close all the way – you can see it here on this slide. There's also a small hole here near the top. It's a bit faded now. The colors used to be much brighter.

▶ 31

Patrick: If you use PowerPoint to present your prized possession, a picture or two can be helpful, especially if your possession is small or has features that are difficult to see. Check the PowerPoint tips on page 43. Then watch Sophie to see how she uses pictures to help her present her diary.

Sophie: I'd like to share this very special possession with you. As you can see, it's pretty small, so it fits easily into my bag. However, it's also around an inch thick because it has 250 pages. I love the cover. Can you see? It's made of blue silk cloth, which feels really smooth, and it has a beautiful oriental design with bamboo trees and pagodas. Here, on the edge and on the corners, it's brown leather. It's difficult to see, but here on the leather there are butterflies.

▶ 32

Patrick: Sophie showed three slides with pictures. Did you mark the same number of pictures in her script? Did she show them in the same places you marked? Remember, pictures on PowerPoint slides should be large and clear, like Sophie's, so they're easy for everyone to see. We'll provide more tips on using pictures and visuals in later units.

Unit 4 Expansion activities

▶ 33

Emma: Hi everyone. I'm Emma. I'll be your guide today. Let's first practice different types of openers and closers to help you feel more confident using them. Watch Grace, Ben, and Sophie introduce their memorable experience. Notice the type of opener they each use.

Grace: Good morning. A wise person once said, "The most memorable experiences in life are the unplanned and unexpected ones." I agree, and today I'd like to tell you about a very memorable experience I recently had that was both unplanned and unexpected.

Ben: Hello everyone. I'd like to ask you a simple question: What is your most memorable summer vacation? Today, I'd like to tell you about my most memorable summer vacation and why it was so important to me.

Sophie: Hi. I'm Sophie, and it's good to speak with you today. We all have many different experiences in life, but most of us only remember a few – the experiences that are really special. This morning, I want to share with you an important experience in my life and how it has changed me.

 34

Emma: Did you notice that all three speakers used a different type of opener? Grace used a quotation about unplanned memorable experiences. Ben's opener was a question to get the audience thinking about vacations. And Sophie made a general comment about experiences, using expressions like *we all* and *most of us*. Now, watch the speakers end their presentations. Notice what type of closer they each use.

Grace: So, now you know all about my exciting, surprising, first experience meeting a real live rock star. As I said, it gave me a different view of famous people. So, I suggest that if you ever see a famous person somewhere, in a shop or restaurant, say hello, talk to them, and remember that even though they're famous, they're still just human, like us.

Ben: To sum up, that summer when I was 15 was a really memorable time for me. Of course, I earned money to buy things that I wanted, and I also enjoyed walking around outside all day. But most of all, that summer is special because I learned a lot about hard work and responsibility. Thank you.

Sophie: To conclude, for me, the homestay I did in Spain was one of the best experiences I've had in my life. Yes, it was difficult, but I did a lot of new things and met so many wonderful people. In fact, I'm sure the new friends I made will come and visit me here in the near future.

 35

Emma: So again, all three speakers ended in a different way. Grace made a suggestion to the audience. Ben emphasized what he learned from his summer job. And Sophie offered some thoughts about the future. So which closer do you like the best?

 36

Emma: In the **Developing presentation techniques** section of Unit 4, you noticed that Sophie wasn't speaking so effectively. Now, watch Grace and Ben. What advice would you give them to improve their voice power?

Grace: This experience happened to me a few years ago, and it was the first time I met someone famous. One day, my best friend Donna and I were at a trendy diner called Johnny's for lunch. We were sitting at the counter, just eating our burgers and fries and talking about our classes at school, when the lead singer of our favorite rock band walked in! It was Jack Thomas from the Outsiders. We couldn't believe it. It was so amazing!

Ben: It was when I was 15 that I got my very first summer job, at a golf course driving range near my house. In fact, my dad often played golf there, and he knew the manager, George Olsen. So, Mr. Olsen agreed to hire me for work four days a week. He said I could start work the next day at 9 a.m. I remember that morning, when I rode my bicycle to the golf course. I was pretty nervous because it was my first job, but I was also really thrilled to earn my own money.

 37

Emma: Grace and Ben both had problems. Grace spoke too softly, so it was hard to hear her. She should speak louder. She also said *um* and *uh* a lot. That makes her sound unprepared. Now, Ben spoke so fast it was difficult to follow him. He needs to slow down. He should also pause slightly between phrases and sentences to sound more natural and to give the audience time to understand. Did you have similar advice?

 38

Emma: In Unit 1, we pointed out that you don't need to memorize your entire presentation. Instead, use note cards. However, your note cards must be easy for you to read. Watch Grace using her note card. Does she have any problems?

Grace: This experience happened to me a few years ago, and it was the first time I met someone famous. One day, my best friend Donna and I were at a trendy diner called Johnny's for lunch. We were sitting at the counter, just eating our burgers and fries and talking about our classes at school, when the lead singer of our favorite rock band walked in! It was Jack Thomas from the Outsiders.

 39

Emma: You saw that Grace had trouble reading her note card, so she had to hold it close to her eyes. That's because her writing was very small and the lines were only single spaced, so she couldn't find the keywords quickly. Now, watch Grace using a new note card and notice the difference.

Grace: This experience happened to me a few years ago, and it was the first time I met someone famous. One day, my best friend Donna and I were at a trendy diner called Johnny's for lunch. We were sitting at the counter, just eating our burgers and fries and talking about our classes at school, when the lead singer of our favorite rock band walked in! It was Jack Thomas from the Outsiders.

40

Emma: This time, Grace was much more effective. She could find the keywords quickly on her note card, then make eye contact again with the audience. That's because her writing was larger and the lines were double-spaced. Remember, note cards are useful only when you can read them easily.

 41

Emma: In your presentation, you may want to include a few slides with pictures or other information, like Patrick did. Remember the tip from page 55: Less is more!

That means don't include too much text or too many pictures on one slide. Now, watch two versions of Patrick's introduction and notice how he shows his information in each one.

Patrick (Versions 1 and 2): Hello everyone. A tropical island, my dad, the sea, a turtle, a test. What do these things have in common? Well, they are all part of one of the most memorable experiences I've had in my life. Today I'd like to tell you about that experience.

 42

Emma: In the first version, Patrick showed the title and all the pictures from his mystery list on the same slide, so it was difficult for us to know where to look when he was speaking. In the second version, Patrick showed us only one picture at a time, so it was easier for us to focus our attention. That's what "Less is more" means. Don't put too much on one slide, so your audience can stay focused and involved.

Unit 5 Expansion activities

 43

Jason: Hi, I'm Jason. I'll be your guide today. Let's start with openers and closers to help you use them effectively. Watch Grace, Ben, and Sophie introduce their demonstration topics. Notice what type of opener they each use.

Grace: Hi, everyone. Thanks for coming today. You know, it's a fact that 70 percent of people in their 20s want to lose weight and be fitter. However, most students don't have the time or money to join an expensive fitness club. Well, don't worry! Today, I'm going to teach you how to do a very simple but effective . . .

Ben: Hello everyone. Tell me, would you like to be able to prepare a special birthday lunch for your sweetheart? How about a lovely Mother's Day breakfast for your mom? Yes, me too. Are you a good cook? No, I'm not either. But that's not a problem, because I'm going to show you a simple way to make a heart-shaped . . .

Sophie: Good morning. A proverb I love is: "The best gift costs little money and much thoughtfulness." I always try to remember that when I am thinking of fun, inexpensive, thoughtful birthday or holiday gifts for friends and family. Recently, I made some colorful paper fortune cookies for my best friend at Chinese New Year, and she loved them. So, today, I'd like to tell you a little bit . . .

 44

Jason: You saw how each speaker started in a different way. Grace began with a surprising fact, Ben asked problem-raising questions, and Sophie used an interesting proverb. Now watch their conclusions. Notice what type of closer they each use.

Grace: So now you know a simple, effective exercise that really works. As you saw, you can do it at home, and you don't need much: only a chair, a towel, and some loose clothes. When you get home today, why don't you try the exercise for 10 minutes? Thank you.

Ben: So, that's how to make your own heart-shaped egg at home. As I showed you, it's not complicated. It's just a few simple steps, and you don't need a lot of materials. They'll love it because it's cute and unique, but most of all because you made it yourself and it comes from your heart. Thank you.

Sophie: So, now you know how to make your own colorful paper fortune cookies at home with just a few materials. They can be creative gifts for friends or fun decorations for parties and special occasions. I hope my short demonstration encourages you to share your skills and talents with others. Thank you.

 45

Jason: Again, each speaker ended in a different way. Grace's closer was a call to action. She encouraged the audience to try her exercise. Ben ended by emphasizing how special the heart-shaped egg is. Finally, Sophie passed the mike. She asked the audience to share their own skills for making things. So, which closer do you like the best?

 46

Jason: In the **Developing presentation techniques** section for Unit 5, you learned that a demonstration involves explaining and showing how to do or make something. The presenter can use gestures to show the action in each step. Watch two versions of Emma's demonstration. Which one is easier to follow?

Emma (Version 1): So, let's see how to make the container. To begin with, unscrew the top from the plastic bottle. Make sure you keep the top because you'll need it in a few minutes. OK. Next, use the scissors or the knife to cut all around the plastic bottle, around 4 to 5 centimeters from the top. You should try to cut in a straight line, so there are no sharp or uneven edges. Here, like this. Right. Then, wash and dry the top of the bottle and the screw top. You don't need the rest. It's important to make sure the bottle and the screw top are both clean and completely dry. OK. Now, twist the top of the open food bag and then push it through the bottle so that it comes out the top.

Emma (Version 2): So, let's see how to make the container. To begin with, unscrew the top from the plastic bottle. Make sure you keep the top because you'll need it in a few minutes. OK. Next, use the scissors or knife to cut all around the plastic bottle, about 4 to 5 centimeters from the top. You should try to cut in a straight line, so there are no sharp, uneven edges. Here, like this. Right. Then, wash and dry the top of the bottle and the screw top. You don't need the rest. It's important to make sure the section of the bottle and the screw top are both clean and completely dry. OK. Now, twist the top of the open food bag and push it through the section of the bottle so that it comes out the top.

▶ 47

Jason: In Emma's first version, she didn't use gestures at all, so it was difficult to follow. However, in her second version, Emma added clear gestures for the actions in every step, so we could follow everything easily. Remember, when you demonstrate how to do or make something, clear gestures really help.

▶ 48

Jason: You can also help the audience follow your demonstration by emphasizing key points. Watch Ben's demonstration and notice the expressions he uses to emphasize the important points for the audience.

Ben: OK. Here's how we do it. Boil the egg for 10 minutes and peel it completely. Use the scissors to cut one side of the milk carton into a rectangle that's 20 centimeters long and 8 centimeters wide. Make sure that the short side is not wider than 8 centimeters. Then, fold along the middle of the long side of the rectangle so it makes a V shape, like this. Put the peeled egg in the center of the carton, like this. After that, lay the chopstick on the top of the egg and press down gently. Be careful not to press down too hard or the egg will break. Now, use the rubber bands and tie each end of the chopstick and carton together to hold the egg inside. See? Are there any questions? OK. Be sure to keep the rubber bands in place at least 10 minutes.

▶ 49

Jason: Did you notice that Ben emphasized three key points? He also used a different expression for each key point to make it more interesting for the audience.

▶ 50

Jason: In your demonstration, you may want to show your audience the steps or instructions on slides. Make sure that your slides are easy to read and they focus the audience's attention on key information. Watch two versions of Emma's conclusion. In which version does she use the slides more effectively?

Emma (Version 1): So, that's how to make a simple, reusable storage container to keep everything fresh, save money, and recycle your plastic bottles. As you saw, you don't need a lot of materials, and the six steps only take a few minutes. Just keep in mind the few key points I mentioned, and you'll have no trouble. I encourage you to try it for yourself at home and stop buying all those re-sealable bags. Thank you.

Emma (Version 2): So, that's how to make a simple, reusable storage container to keep everything fresh, save money, and recycle your plastic bottles. As you saw, you don't need a lot of materials, and the six steps only take a few minutes. Just keep in mind the few key points I mentioned, and you'll have no trouble. I encourage you to try it for yourself at home and stop buying all those re-sealable bags. Thank you.

▶ 51

Jason: In Emma's first version, she put all the instructions and key points on one slide. Twelve items on one slide is too many. And we didn't have enough time to read it. She also didn't highlight keywords with color or capital letters to focus our attention. However, Emma's second version was more effective. She used two slides, so first we could focus on the instructions and then on the key points. She also highlighted the verbs in blue and capitals. Finally, she gave us time to read the information. Remember these simple PowerPoint tips and your audience will really appreciate it.

Unit 6 Expansion activities

▶ 52

Sophie: Hi everyone. I'll be your guide today. First, let's look at some different types of openers. Watch Emma, Grace, and Ben introduce their movies and TV shows. Notice the type of opener they each use.

Emma: Hello everyone. A 14-year-old boy, a Bengal tiger, a small lifeboat on the Pacific Ocean, a deadly island, and a Canadian interviewer. What do these things have in common? They are all in a popular novel and the best movie of 2012. *Life of Pi* is a magical adventure movie about an Indian boy named Pi, who spends months on a small boat in the ocean with a Bengal tiger.

Grace: Hello everyone. When we think about life on earth in the future, many of us imagine that it will be more difficult, dangerous, and violent than now. Maybe that's why movies like *The Hunger Games* are so popular. *The Hunger Games* is the first of several sci-fi adventure movies based on a popular novel.

Ben: Good afternoon everyone. A popular writer once said, "Fantasy is not an escape from reality. It's a way of understanding it." He was talking about books, but maybe it's also true for television. *Game of Thrones* is a fantasy drama series that is set on the fictional continent of Westeros.

▶ 53

Sophie: Did you notice that each speaker began differently? Emma began with a list, Grace gave a general statement, and finally Ben used an interesting quotation. Now, watch their conclusions to find out what their ratings and recommendations are.

Emma: So what do I think of *Life of Pi*? Overall, I give it three stars out of five for its amazing special effects. I think it's worth seeing, especially in a movie theater or on a big HD screen in a dark room. Thank you.

Grace: So overall, what's my final rating of *The Hunger Games*? I'd give it two thumbs up. I think it's definitely worth watching for its fast-moving plot and great acting. I recommend that you rent it and see it at home with your friends. Thank you.

Ben: So, what's my final rating of *Game of Thrones*? It's absolutely worth watching. I would give it an eight out of 10 for its fascinating plot and stunning scenery. My recommendation is to watch every episode and download any that you miss. Thank you for listening.

 54

Sophie: Each speaker gave a rating and a final recommendation. Notice they also reviewed the main features to explain their ratings. When you give your movie or TV show presentation, remember to include your rating, using a number or stars, and your recommendation to see it – or not!

 55

Sophie: In the **Developing presentation techniques** section of Unit 6, you practiced saying two sections of Jason's presentation with natural sentence stress and phrasing with pauses. Now, watch Jason and compare his version with yours.

Jason: As a child, Clark discovers that he has special powers, and later he tries to find out where he comes from. In his travels, he meets the reporter Lois Lane, and he communicates by hologram with his father, Jor-El. Clark learns that he was sent to Earth to bring hope to mankind.

 56

Sophie: Now watch the second part of Jason's presentation and compare his version with yours.

Jason: *Man of Steel* is set on the planet Krypton and on Earth, including the United States and Canada. The movie covers Superman's life from infancy to his 30s. The movie tells the story of Superman's origins – how he becomes Superman. At the beginning, Krypton is dying, so its leader, Jor-El, sends his baby son, Kal-El, to Earth. Kal-El is adopted by kindly farmers in Kansas, and they name him Clark.

 57

Sophie: Making and using clear note cards can give you more confidence when you present. However, you still need to practice a lot before you give your presentation. Watch two versions of Patrick's presentation and notice how he uses his note cards in each version.

Patrick (Version 1): *The Walking Dead* is a horror drama series that takes place in America – sorry – America in the near future. The main character is Rick Grimes, a sheriff who – a sheriff who wakes up after being in a coma for several months and discovers that zombies have taken over the world. He goes to Atlanta to search for his wife and son and narrowly escapes the zombies. Rick – Rick then meets – Rick finds his wife and son and other survivors. Together, they fight against the zombies and also against other groups of survivors, who will do anything to stay alive.

Patrick (Version 2): *The Walking Dead* is a horror drama series that takes place in America in the near future. The main character is Rick Grimes, a sheriff who wakes up after being in a coma for several months and discovers that zombies have taken over the world. He goes to Atlanta to search for his wife and son and narrowly escapes the zombies. Rick then meets another survivor and they go to a camp, where Rick finds his wife and son and other survivors. Together, they fight against the zombies and also against other groups of survivors, who will do anything to stay alive.

 58

Sophie: In Patrick's first version, he didn't practice enough. He had to look at his note cards a lot. His cards were also in the wrong order. However, the second time, Patrick was better prepared. He kept good eye contact with the audience.

 59

Sophie: One way to make sure your PowerPoint slides are attractive, clear, and easy to read is to choose fonts and colors carefully. Watch two versions of Jason's introduction and focus on his slides. Which version do you prefer?

Jason (Versions 1 and 2): *Man of Steel* is different from other Superman movies, and there are a lot of things I liked about it. First, the plot is easy to follow, without confusing flashbacks. As well, the visual effects are absolutely spectacular! The battle between Superman and Zod is awesome. Finally, the acting is excellent. Henry Cavill does a great job playing Clark Kent as he struggles to find his life purpose. He's also a very believable superhero. Russell Crowe also gives a moving performance as Jor-El.

 60

Sophie: In both versions, Jason's slide has the same information. However, in the first version, his slide has lots of different colors and fonts. That makes it confusing. In Jason's second version, he uses only two colors and he uses two easy-to-read fonts. That makes it simple and clear. Remember, when you use PowerPoint, don't mix too many different fonts and colors. Remember: Less is more!